Proclaiming in a New Season

A **Practical Guide** to **Catholic Preaching** for the **New Evangelization**

Peter Lovrick

LITURGICAL PRESS

Collegeville, Minnesota

www.litpress.org

RECYCLED
Paper made from
recycled material
FSC® C103567
FSC
www.fsc.org

© 2016 Novalis Publishing Inc.

Cover design and layout: Audrey Wells
Cover photograph: iStockphoto

Published in the United States by
Liturgical Press
Collegeville, MN 56321
www.litpress.org

ISBN: 978-0-8146-4605-2 (paperback)
ISBN: 978-0-8146-4629-8 (ebook)

Printed in Canada.

Contents

Foreword

"Put your time in the homily, your money in the music, and greet the people at the door of the church." This wise advice was recently given to the priests of my diocese by an experienced Catholic pastor who has thought carefully about what is needed to be sure that a parish is a vibrant faith community. Many years earlier, I had asked a non-Catholic expert on contemporary religious practice, who was particularly familiar with those who had left the practice of the faith, to speak to the priests on his findings. He noted that what people wanted was good homilies that gave them spiritual nourishment for the week, and good music, and a spirit of welcome. It is interesting that two people from very different backgrounds, who have both thought deeply about what is needed for a vibrant faith community, gave basically the same advice: be attentive to homilies, music and welcome.

I have noticed over my 18 years as a bishop that when parishioners have spoken to me of their concerns about the life of the Church, they frequently place particular emphasis on the need for good homilies. They are delighted when they experience them, and discouraged when they do not. Sometimes they go off to non-Catholic churches that emphasize preaching. It is not surprising that Pope Francis devoted a very large part of *The Joy of the Gospel* to the need for good homilies. And recently, the Vatican issued a Directory on Homiletics, to help improve preaching.

Deacon Peter Lovrick is responsible for our homiletics program at St. Augustine's Seminary in Toronto. He is eminently qualified for this work and has developed many creative initiatives to help improve preaching. I am delighted that he has gathered together in this book some of the insights he has gained after years of homiletical study, teaching and practice, and is sharing them more widely in this book.

If we are to care pastorally for those who are gathered around the altar of the Lord, and for those as well who are scattered and who no longer practise the faith, we need to focus on effective preaching, rooted in scripture and in the living faith of the Church, as well as in the lives of the people.

I am confident that *Proclaiming in a New Season: A Practical Guide to Catholic Preaching for the New Evangelization* will be a great blessing for those who have received the mission of preaching, especially in the context of the Eucharist, and will help them to become better preachers. That will also, of course, be a blessing for all those whose lives are enriched by their preaching, and who are challenged, guided and encouraged in their life of discipleship.

Thomas Cardinal Collins
Toronto, Ontario
June 2015

Preface

The ministry of preaching is precious. St. Paul tells us why:

> For, "Everyone who calls on the name of the Lord shall be saved." But how are they to call on one in whom they have not believed? And how are they to believe in one of whom they have never heard? And how are they to hear without someone to proclaim him? And how are they to proclaim him unless they are sent? As it is written, "How beautiful are the feet of those who bring good news!" (Rom 10:13-15)

St. Paul makes a promise to the world and issues a challenge to the Church. The promise is that God extends his offer of salvation through Jesus Christ to everyone. The challenge is that the Church must send preachers to announce that Good News.

That is, preachers go out to proclaim the Word in good season and bad in the name of the Church rather than in their own names. They evangelize, bringing converts to the Church, and preach to the family in the Church, calling it to ever-deeper conversion.

What does it mean, though, to preach in the name of the Church? What does the Church call its preachers to do when it sends them out? Preaching has meant different things in different times. The Church has made it very clear what it means in our times. Much work has been done on a homiletic renewal since the Second Vatican Council (1962–65). The popes have consistently underlined a call for good preaching based on principles fundamental to a particular vision of preaching that the Church holds out to its preachers today. That vision is a theology of preaching informed by the homiletic practice of the Church Fathers. It does not imitate patristic preaching, but rather is inspired by it to meet the needs of the Church and the world to which it proposes the Gospel.

When the popes tell us that the quality of preaching needs to be improved – immediately and urgently – preachers respond to that call by first understanding just what that theology of preaching, that vision, is. Equipped with that understanding, they can then articulate the marks of outstanding preaching – those marks that fulfill the calling of the Church. Once they have those marks in place, they can determine practical means to achieve them.

This book is organized to do just that. Part 1 outlines just what the Church is asking for. Part 2 presents methods for delineating and measuring the characteristics of preaching that fulfills the Church's vision. Part 3 discusses the practical things preachers can do to accomplish those goals. A case study for putting together a homily based on the principles of this book is available as a free PDF download from this link: http://novalis. uberflip.com/i/623299-appendix-proclaiming-in-a-new-season-final.

How beautiful – indeed, how precious – is the preacher to the mission of the Church. This book is meant to bring that mission into focus, laying out the fruit of the Church's renewal of the homily for modern times.

Part 1

Is There a Problem?

Preaching is indispensable to the life of the Church. Her mission to evangelize depends upon it. Her vocation to nourish the faithful requires it. Her calling to praise God rests upon it. To effectively accomplish its purpose, preaching needs to respond to the needs of the time. Preaching at one time is not the same as preaching at another. The world changes, the experience of the listeners changes, and the way they listen changes. The message of the Gospel is timeless, but the way that message is delivered depends upon time and place. The Church has called for a renewal of preaching ever since the Second Vatican Council. That call has become more critical in the 21st century as the Church embarks on the New Evangelization. Yet, the Church also tells its preachers that there is a serious problem with Catholic preaching, requiring thoughtful attention. Identifying the problem is the first step in developing some clarity for preachers as to just what they should be doing. So – what is the problem? One way to get at it is to look at what the people in the pews, priests and deacons, and the bishops of the world tell us.

What do the people in the pews say?

The American bishops, in the introduction to their 2013 document on preaching, *Preaching the Mystery of Faith*, make the following observation:

> We are also aware that in survey after survey over the past year, the people of God have called for more powerful and inspiring preaching. A steady diet of tepid or poorly prepared homilies is often cited as a cause for discouragement on the part of laity and even leading some to turn away from the Church. (2)

Paying attention to how homilies are heard is the basis of effective preaching. In *Preaching the Mystery of Faith*, the American bishops emphasize that the problem they are responding to is not an isolated one. The frequently repeated feedback is that so many people find homilies to be uninspired and thus without power. The bishops diagnose the cause of tepid homilies as poor preparation, and the effects as discouragement and loss of connection with the Church. Alarm bells deserve attention, and the bishops have sounded the alarm that the reception of preaching has serious consequences. The *National Catholic Reporter* observed that if ex-Catholics were considered as a group, they would be the third-largest denomination in the United States (CNN Belief Blog, March 30, 2012). PewResearch reported that roughly 10% of the American population is made up of ex-Catholics (PewResearch, retrieved November 12, 2014). The bishops are not suggesting that preaching drove these people to abandon the Church. There are many complicated and diverse reasons for the loss of faith. They are saying, however, that these people did not hear anything convincing or compelling enough to give hope, power and inspiration so they would stay.

The bishops note that "survey after survey" has shown this problem to be with us for some time. One survey conducted by the National Opinion Research Center in 2001 noted that whereas 36% of Protestants rated the preaching they heard as excellent, only 18% of Catholics would say the same (Andrew Greeley, *The New York Times*, March 3, 2004). More recently, Dr. Karla Bellinger published her research on how young people respond to Catholic preaching. Her survey of over 650 teenagers in urban and suburban Catholic high schools across the United States showed that for whatever reason, the Catholic preaching they heard at Mass had little or no impact. Of those who attended Mass regularly, 15% were enthusiastic. Of the rest, most were ambivalent, while 38.1% stated flatly that they would not recommend the homilies they heard to anyone (Bellinger, 21). Dr. Bellinger noted one significant reason for this underwhelming effect: "There was a constant written comment – the Sunday homily was targeted at the 'older folks'" (Bellinger, 94). In other words, the homily did not connect with young Catholics and consequently, in Bellinger's work, received an overall assessment of a low C- from these listeners (Bellinger, 111). This does not necessarily mean that the homilies they heard were somehow poor; it simply reports that yet another constituent group of listeners is neither inspired nor motivated by what they hear from the pulpit.

What do priests and deacons say?

Interestingly enough, priests and deacons also see a problem with preaching today. Several independent surveys in Canada demonstrate that few clerics find the current state of preaching excellent. A 2008 survey of the priests of the Archdiocese of Toronto showed that whereas only 1% thought the state of preaching excellent, and 7% good, over 70% thought it needed some to significant improvement. By far, the biggest problem, according to these priests, is poor delivery, followed by superficial content. Similar questions were asked at an international conference on Catholic preaching at St. Augustine's Seminary in 2014. While about 23% thought that the state of Catholic preaching was good, 53% said it needed improvement, and about 15% thought it needed significant improvement. The clergy at that conference also identified poor delivery as the primary problem, followed by a lack of clarity. Only 9% of the priests and deacons in the diocese of St. Catharines,Ontario, evaluated contemporary Catholic preaching as good; none thought it excellent. They indicated that the biggest problem is that much preaching is disconnected from the needs of the assembly, closely followed by poor delivery. A survey of clergy in Winnipeg (2015) showed that only 7% thought the preaching in North America was excellent, and 30% thought it good. Separate studies of permanent deacons show the same results. Only 20% of the deacons in the diocese of Kingston, Ontario, rate current Catholic preaching as good. They, too, identified poor delivery and a disconnect from the assembly as the main issues. The more than 70% response from the permanent deacons surveyed in the Archdiocese of Toronto identifying preaching as needing some to significant improvement highlighted flat, boring or incomprehensible delivery as the most significant problem.

What do the bishops say?

Both the American and Canadian bishops have identified good preaching as a priority in their programs for priestly formation. The United

States Conference of Catholic Bishops' document spells out clearly what the bishops expect.

Pastoral formation needs to emphasize the proclamation of God's Word, which indeed is the first task of the priest. This proclamation ministry is aimed at the conversion of sinners and is rooted in the seminarian/preacher's ability to listen deeply to the lived experiences and realities of the faithful. This listening is followed by the preacher's ability to interpret those lived experiences in the light of Sacred Scripture and the Church's Tradition. Understanding this intersection of God's Word and human experiences, the seminarian/preacher initiates a lifelong mission and ministry of bringing God's Word to the world through preaching and teaching. This requires that the seminarian couple the deepest convictions of faith with the development of his communication skills so that God's Word may be effectively expressed. (*Program of Priestly Formation*, 239)

This is a tall order, requiring preachers to listen, pray, study and communicate. It is not something that just happens. Consequently, the bishops declare,

Homiletics should occupy a prominent place in the core curriculum and be integrated into the entire course of studies. In addition to the principles of biblical interpretation, catechesis, and communications theory, seminarians should also learn the practical skills needed to communicate the Gospel as proclaimed by the Church in an effective and appropriate manner. (215)

The Canadian bishops, in their *Program for Priestly Formation*, also have high expectations.

The *ministry of the word* reveals itself in the relationship of the priest to the word of God spoken among the People of God, enabling them to be prophets in the world. *Presbyterorum Ordinis* affirms that priests, as co-workers with their bishops, have as their primary duty the proclamation of the Gospel of God to all (*see PO*, 4). For priests to be faithful to the proclamation of the Gospel in preaching, catechetics and education, they require an intimate, contemplative and scholarly knowledge of the Sacred

Scriptures and Tradition, as well as hearts and minds attuned to the joys and sorrows of men and women today. (19)

Like their American counterparts, the Canadian bishops call for their preachers to bring a personal and prayerful, in addition to scholarly, understanding of scripture to a pastoral, intuitive and empathetic understanding of the people who listen to them.

How well are these expectations being met? In 2002, the Catholic Association of Teachers of Homiletics (CATH) published a white paper, *The State of Homiletics in the Seminaries and Graduate Schools of Theology in the United States*, in which they assess just how well the bishops' call for an emphasis on homiletics training has been realized. After surveying formation programs for ordination across the US, the CATH white paper concludes:

> Since the average M.Div. degree requires well over 100 credits of study, it would be difficult to argue that homiletics occupies "a prominent place" in most seminarians' training. Regrettably, the lack of prominence first noted in 1992 persists. (Section I.A.)

Both the American and Canadian bishops report that a frequent concern that crosses their desks has to do with preaching. The bishops have raised these concerns in a collaborative way at extraordinary synods.

The 2008 synod on the Word of God in the Life and Mission of the Church naturally took up the homily as an expression of the Gospel. That synod's *Instrumentum Laboris* states:

> A paradox is increasingly evident: the faithful's hunger for the Word of God is not always receiving an adequate response in the preaching of the Church's pastors, because of a deficiency in seminary preparation or pastoral practice. (No. 27)

In this way, the question of inadequate preaching became an explicit topic for the synod, but just what did this question mean? In what way had Catholic preaching become increasingly inadequate? What, in fact, were the bishops calling for?

Bishop Gerald Frederick Kicanas of Tucson minced no words when he described inadequate preaching this way:

Unfortunately, preaching in our day can lose its savor, become formulaic and uninspired leaving the hearer empty. (*Third General Congregation*, Tuesday, 7 October 2008)

Turning this sentence around shows what this particular bishop wanted from his preachers. For him, good preaching requires

1. savour,
2. creativity, and
3. inspiration.

The terms imply a great deal. Savour suggests preaching that is both rich and attractive. Creativity, as opposed to the formulaic, implies preaching that is alive and organic. Inspiration speaks of a movement in the soul triggered by preaching that changes lives. This vision of preaching is already a tall order, but the bishops had much more to say.

Cardinal Stanislaw Dziwisz, Archbishop of Krakow, repeated *Instrumentum Laboris'* diagnosis of the state of preaching and expanded on its claim that the root of the problem was in poor seminary training.

The elementary problem lies in the fact that this Word needs fervent witnesses ready to share with others the truth that changed their lives. The seminary formation period is a particular time for the preparation of such witnesses. But sometimes it seems that candidates to priesthood treat the texts of the Sacred Scriptures as an object of study without taking into account its spiritual dimension. For them, the Scripture does not become the Word of their life. The force of the Word, capable of changing man, converting him is not unleashed by the Scripture. (*Sixth General Congregation*, 9 October 2008)

Thus, Cardinal Dziwisz wants his preachers to be passionate witnesses for the bold claim that the Word of God changes lives. His language is striking. Good preaching, he insists, needs to unleash the power of scripture in the midst of the assembly. To do that, preachers require something more than an academic approach to exegesis of the Word of God. He calls that essential component "the spiritual dimension."

Seeing the preacher's task as "unleashing the power of scripture" is the antidote to tepid preaching that has no effect because it neither moves nor awakens, and that is neither heard nor remembered. The

12th-century archbishop Baldwin of Canterbury had something remarkable to say about this; the Church has included it in the Office of Readings.

> When this word is preached, in the very act of preaching it gives to its own voice which is heard outwardly a certain power which is perceived inwardly so much so that the dead are brought back to life and by these praises the sons of Abraham are raised from the dead. This word then is alive in the heart of the Father, on the lips of preachers, and in the hearts of those who believe and love him. Since this word is so truly alive, undoubtedly it is full of power. It is powerful in creation, powerful in the government of the universe, powerful in the redemption of the world. For what is more powerful, more effective? Who shall speak of its power; who shall make all its praises heard? It is powerful in what it accomplishes, powerful when preached. It does not come back empty; it bears fruit in all to whom it is sent. It is powerful and more piercing than any two-edged sword when it is believed and loved. (Friday, Thirtieth Week in Ordinary Time)

Any preacher who walks to the ambo with this mindset cannot help but preach differently from someone who does not have it. Such a preacher is not conducting an academic exercise, promoting a personal agenda or delivering only exegesis or catechesis, but is standing on holy ground as a personal vehicle for an act of power that, as Cardinal Dziwisz calls for, changes lives.

Although *Instrumentum Laboris* traced the causes of inadequate preaching to deficient seminary training and pastoral practice, Cardinal Marc Ouellet was concerned to point out the effects. After underscoring the problem of inadequate preaching, he made a bold claim as to what poor preaching really means for the Church since the Second Vatican Council.

> Despite the renewal that the homily was made subject of the Council, we still feel great lack of satisfaction on the part of many faithful with regards to the ministry of preaching. In part, this lack of satisfaction explains why many Catholics turned toward other groups and religions. (*Report Before the Discussion of the General Reporter*, 6 October 2008)

Cardinal Ouellet's report at the synod underlined the need for greater attention to preaching. He asked the bishops,

> How can we help homilists place the life and Word in relationship with this eschatological event that surges in the heart of the assembly? The homily must reach spiritual "depth", that is to say, the Christology of Holy Scriptures. How can we avoid the tendency towards moralism and cultivate the calling to a decision of faith? (*Report*, October 8 2012)

This vision of the homily calls for preaching that puts what Christ does in the centre, rather than moral exhortation, with the ultimate goal of eliciting a decision – a decision to choose Christ.

The stakes are high. Unleashing the power of the Word through preaching is meant to accomplish a high purpose. It is meant to make a real and significant difference in the listener. Poor or lukewarm preaching is not, however, just the absence of that. Poor preaching is not just a potentially powerful moment that has been regretfully rendered powerless. It is not simply that poor preaching results in a flat, uninspired moment during liturgy. Cardinal Ouellet gives inadequate preaching a far more serious implication by connecting it directly to a hemorrhaging of the faithful from the Church. This dramatic claim was endorsed by Bishop Desiderius Rwoma of Tanzania the next day:

> If we speak of people being lukewarm concerning matters of the faith and the phenomenon of religious sects which are spreading at an alarming speed in many parts of the world, the causes for this can possibly be traced back to a lack of good and proper preaching from the part of ministers. (*Fourth General Congregation*, 7 October 2008)

But this begs the question – just what is good and proper preaching? What does the Church want of its preachers at this time in its history?

What does the Church want from its preachers?

The Catholic Church circles the globe, extending through time and into the reality that is beyond the temporal. That great family, that great house, fosters much diversity expressed through charism, personality, calling and gift. Many spiritualities, whether Franciscan, Dominican,

Jesuit, Basilian or any other, are legitimate expressions of what it means to be Catholic. Yet, if a spirituality crosses out of the parameters of what it means to be Catholic, then it is something else, something other than Catholic.

Grace builds upon nature, and Catholics are called to express who they are, to express their own identities – but within the framework of the identity of the family. So, too, does preaching. The Church does not call for cookie-cutter preachers, delivering uniform homilies throughout the world irrespective of place, time and assembly. Preachers are encouraged to be who they are, to build upon their strengths, talents and character – their own personhood – yet to do all this within the parameters, the framework of what the Church wants from preaching.

The Church has clearly told its preachers what that calling means in modern times. That message, starting with the Second Vatican Council, has been refined and polished, always moved forward, not turned back, through the successive pontificates. A look at what the Church has said under each of the popes since the council brings the calling of preaching for the times into sharp focus.

Blessed Pope Paul VI

One of the great fruits of the Second Vatican Council was the renewed emphasis on the Word of God. Scripture was given a higher profile. The Old Testament, along with the Gospels, the Epistles and the psalms, were proclaimed at Mass. *Sacrosanctum Concilium* (The Constitution on the Sacred Liturgy) provided a vision of preaching that was to unfold and become increasingly clarified over the following decades:

> The sermon, moreover, should draw its content mainly from scriptural and liturgical sources, and its character should be that of a proclamation of God's wonderful works in the history of salvation, the mystery of Christ, ever made present and active within us, especially in the celebration of the liturgy. (35)

The Council fathers laid it out for preachers. Preaching was to be based on scripture and liturgy, not on themes or topics that did not refer to scripture or referred to it only in passing, as a springboard to the preacher's own agenda. The focus of preaching was to be on what

God does, not on what Cardinal Ouellet called "moralism." The effect of preaching was to uncover the presence of Christ "ever made present" in our lives and particularly in liturgy. They also made a significant call for a repositioning of preaching.

> By means of the homily the mysteries of the faith and the guiding principles of the Christian life are expounded from the sacred text, during the course of the liturgical year; the homily, therefore, is to be highly esteemed as part of the liturgy itself. (52)

Before the council, at the moment of preaching, the priest would remove his maniple (a long, narrow strip of silk worn over the left arm during the liturgy), leave the sanctuary to climb into a pulpit, and preach a sermon that could have nothing to do with the readings of that Mass, but rather followed a catechetical program based on the creed, the Our Father, the virtues or other topics. It was as if there was a pause in the Mass, and that the preacher concluded his sermon with the sign of the cross to get the Mass back on track again. The fathers at Vatican II envisaged preaching as fully integrated with the liturgy. The renewal of the Mass, in fact, divided it into the Liturgy of the Word and the Liturgy of the Eucharist. To emphasize this integration, the Congregation for Sacraments and Divine Worship specifically discouraged preachers from making the sign of the cross after preaching.

> Generally speaking it is inadvisable to continue such customs because they have their origin in preaching outside Mass. The homily is part of the liturgy; the people have already blessed themselves and received the greeting at the beginning of Mass. It is better then, not to have a repetition before or after the homily. (*Notitiae*, v. 9 [1978], 178, DOL-1432; note R8)

The Council was calling for the Church's preachers to preach in a different way. Pope Paul VI reminded his preachers just how seriously he wanted them to take this calling. In *Ecclesiam Suam*, he stressed that preaching must take priority:

> In effect, the apostolate and sacred preaching are more or less synonymous terms. Preaching is the primary apostolate. Our ministry, Venerable brethren, is before all else the ministry of the Word. We are well aware of this, but it is good to remind

ourselves of it at the present time so as to give the right orientation to our pastoral activities. We must return to the study, not of human eloquence of empty rhetoric, but of the genuine art of proclaiming the Word of God. (90)

This elevation of preaching and the ministry of the Word "before all else" put things in perspective, especially to clerics who, faced with complex demands on their time, put homily preparation somewhat lower on their to-do list. It was not a new idea. The Church declared an exalted place for preaching at the fifth session of the Council of Trent:

> But seeing that the preaching of the Gospel is no less necessary to the Christian commonwealth than the reading thereof; and whereas this is the principal duty of bishops, the same holy Synod hath resolved and decreed, that all bishops, archbishops, primates and all other prelates of the churches be bound personally – if they be not lawfully hindered – to preach the holy Gospel of Jesus Christ. (17 June 1546)

Although not a new idea, what Pope Paul does is clarify the matter lest anyone interpret it to mean that preaching as the primary apostolate is really a matter for the bishops alone. He declares in *Presbyterorum Ordinis* (*Decree on the Ministry and Life of Priests*) that

> The people of God are joined together primarily by the word of the living God. And rightfully they expect this from their priests. Since no one can be saved who does not first believe, priests, as co-workers with their bishops, have the primary duty of proclaiming the Gospel of God to all. (4)

The ministry of the Word is primary because it is through that ministry that the people hear, believe and are joined in that glorious communion called Church. In *Mysterium Fidei*, this pope tells us in a significant pronouncement why that is the case. Christ is, writes the Pope, sacramentally present in the sacrifice of the Mass. He is there, body and blood, soul and divinity in the transubstantiation of the bread and wine. But he is also there in another way, in the Word and in the preaching of the Word.

> In still another very genuine way, He is present in the Church as she preaches, since the Gospel which she proclaims is the

word of God, and it is only in the name of Christ, the Incarnate Word of God, and by His authority and with His help that it is preached, so that there might be "one flock resting secure in one shepherd." (36)

Christ is really present in the Eucharist, but if he is also in a "very genuine way" present in the preaching, this makes preaching, as an extension of the proclamation of the Word, a sacramental moment. At Mass, commissioned readers proclaim the first and second readings, and a cantor sings the responsorial psalm, but at the moment of the Gospel, the ordained comes to the ambo. The assembly stands, the deacon is blessed, the Book of Gospels is incensed and the Gospel is proclaimed. It is set apart from the proclamation of scripture that just preceded it. So, too, preaching at a Mass is a liturgical function that comes with ordination, setting it off from other kinds of preaching.

All of this requires preachers to come to the ambo knowing that they are engaged in a sacramental act. Bishop Ken Untener made a powerful observation about this reality:

In the homily, the homilist is pointed in a different direction than is the celebrant in the Eucharistic prayer.

- In the Eucharistic prayer, the celebrant "stands facing God" and speaks to God on behalf of the people.

- In the homily, the homilist "stands facing the people" and speaks to the people on behalf of God. (9)

Preachers are on holy ground. They speak on behalf of God, yet speak with, through and from their own lives, gifts, talents, experience and faith. Pope Paul asked for preaching that "expresses the profound faith of the sacred minister and is impregnated with love" (*Evangelii Nuntiandi*, 43). He outlines the characteristics of this kind of preaching:

The faithful assembled as a Paschal Church, celebrating the feast of the Lord present in their midst, expect much from this preaching, and will greatly benefit from it provided that it is simple, clear, direct, well-adapted, profoundly dependent on Gospel teaching and faithful to the magisterium, animated by a balanced apostolic ardor coming from its own characteristic nature, full of hope, fostering belief, and productive of peace and unity. (43)

These few beautiful lines set out a program of preaching that the following pontiffs expounded on and deepened over the years. Pope Paul observes that a renewed vision of preaching also means a renewed vision of preachers. He tells preachers what he has in mind in an oft-quoted passage from *Evangelii Nuntiandi* (On Evangelization in the Modern World). Whereas preachers at different times and in different places have been teachers or heralds, this pope says that what the Church needs in modern times is witnesses.

As we said recently to a group of lay people, "Modern man listens more willingly to witnesses than to teachers, and if he does listen to teachers, it is because they are witnesses." (41)

Just what, however, does all this mean, and how does a preacher live up to it? For that, a compass or a model is necessary. That model is patristic preaching. Pope Benedict XVI points out in the post-synodal apostolic exhortation *Verbum Domini* that the council Fathers looked to the Fathers of the Church for a prayerful approach to the Word that unveiled the senses of scripture. He concludes, "the Council thus sought to reappropriate the great patristic tradition which had always recommended approaching the Scripture in dialogue with God" (86). Earlier, Pope St. John Paul II was also careful to point out the inspiration of patristic preaching for a modern preacher. "His words are to be imbibed with pastoral charity, he chooses them wisely and develops an appropriate style, drawing inspiration from the great masters, especially the Fathers of the Church" (*Apostolorum Successores*, 121). It is not that patristic preaching is to be imitated or repeated; rather, it helps inform the modern preacher's practice, bringing into focus the vision of preaching that emerges from the council. Fr. Robert Waznak demonstrates the connection to one patristic preacher in particular: Origen.

It was Origen (185–254) who for the first time in Christian usage supplied a definition to the word "homily." He called his thirty-nine discourses on Luke *homiliai*. They (1) were preached in liturgy, (2) had a prophetic quality, (3) were based on a running or continuous exposition of the biblical text, and (4) were conversational in tone. (4)

These are the characteristics that emerge from *Sacrosanctum Concilium* and from the writings of Pope Paul VI. They come into sharper focus in succeeding pontificates.

Pope St. John Paul II

Early in his pontificate, Pope John Paul II issued *Catechesi Tradendae*, his post-synodal apostolic exhortation following the fourth general assembly of the Synod of Bishops in 1977 on catechesis in modern times. He makes some striking points about the homily in that document. The pope stresses that catechesis has three dimensions: word, memorial and witness-doctrine, and celebration and commitment in living, all of which come together in different settings (47). He then turns his attention to the particular setting of the homily in the Eucharistic assembly.

> Respecting the specific nature and proper cadence of this setting, the homily takes up again the journey of faith put forward by catechesis, and brings it to its natural fulfillment. At the same time it encourages the Lord's disciples to begin anew each day their spiritual journey in truth, adoration and thanksgiving. Accordingly, one can say that catechetical teaching too finds its source and its fulfillment in the Eucharist, within the whole circle of the liturgical year. Preaching, centered upon the Bible texts, must then in its own way make it possible to familiarize the faithful with the whole of the mysteries of the faith and with the norms of Christian living. Much attention must be given to the homily: it should be neither too long nor too short; it should always be carefully prepared, rich in substance and adapted to the hearers, and reserved to ordained ministers. The homily should have its place not only in every Sunday and feast-day Eucharist, but also in the celebration of baptisms, penitential liturgies, marriages and funerals. This is one of the benefits of the liturgical renewal. (48)

To catechize or not to catechize has been the dividing line. One position is that the re-visioning of preaching in the council clearly calls for a homiletic that gets away from a methodical teaching of catechetical points and focuses on the renewed prominence of scripture in the Mass. Another position holds that the faithful desperately need to be catechized, made better acquainted with Church teachings and brought onto the same page. The argument goes that most of the faithful will not attend special catechetical events and so have only those few minutes at Mass to get the story straight. Pope John Paul II shows that this is a bogus division. The two positions are not mutually exclusive. Both are essential and both are brought together in the re-visioning of the homily. Preaching, which "takes up the journey of faith put forward by catechesis," is to be "centered upon the Biblical texts." In this way, the catechesis does not drive the homily as something scheduled ahead of time, disconnected from the prayers and readings of the Mass. Rather, it emerges from the readings of the Mass and supports the message of the prayers and readings for that liturgical event. That message is to be brought to bear on contemporary experience:

> The purpose of the homily is to explain to the faithful the Word of God proclaimed in the readings and to apply its message to the present. Accordingly, the homily is to be given by the priest or the deacon. (*Inaestimabile Donum*, 3)

It is also significant that the Pope, while urging that a homily be neither too long nor too short in delivery, also calls for a homily that requires significant preparation so it can be both rich and well adapted.

The beautiful introduction to the second edition of the lectionary, published in 1981, brings together the thinking of Pope Paul VI and Pope John Paul II on the homily. Sections 24 and 25 are valuable guidelines for any preacher.

In the Lectionary	In Other Documents	Characteristic of Preaching
Through the course of the liturgical year the homily sets forth the mysteries of faith and the standards of the Christian life on the basis of the sacred text. (24)	By means of the homily the mysteries of the faith and the guiding principles of the Christian life are expounded from the sacred text, during the course of the liturgical year. *Sacrosanctum Concilium* (52)	Biblical

In the Lectionary	In Other Documents	Characteristic of Preaching
Beginning with the Constitution on the Liturgy, the homily as part of the liturgy of the word has been r epeatedly and strongly recommended and in some cases it is obligatory. (24)	The homily, therefore, is to be highly esteemed as part of the liturgy itself; in fact, at those Masses which are celebrated with the assistance of the people on Sundays and feasts of obligation, it should not be omitted except for a serious reason. *Sacrosanctum Concilium* (52)	Liturgical
As a rule, it is to be given by the one presiding. (24)	Reserved to ordained ministers. Pope John Paul II, *Catechesi Tradendae* (48)	Sacramental
The purpose of the homily at Mass is that the spoken word of God and the liturgy of the Eucharist may together become "a proclamation of God's wonderful work in the history of salvation, the mystery of Christ." (24)	Its character should be that of a proclamation of God's wonderful works in the history of salvation, the mystery of Christ, ever made present and active within us, especially in the celebration of the liturgy.	Christocentric
Through the readings and homily Christ's paschal mystery is proclaimed; through the sacrifice of the Mass it becomes present. Moreover Christ himself is always present and active in the preaching of his Church. (24)	In still another very genuine way, He is present in the Church as she preaches, since the Gospel which she proclaims is the word of God, and it is only in the name of Christ, the Incarnate Word of God, and by His authority and with His help that it is preached, so that there might be "one flock resting secure in one shepherd." Pope Paul VI, *Mysterium Fidei* (36)	Sacramental

➡

In the Lectionary	In Other Documents	Characteristic of Preaching
Whether the homily explains the text of the Sacred Scriptures proclaimed in the readings or some other text of the Liturgy, it must always lead the community of the faithful to celebrate the Eucharist actively "so that they may hold fast in their lives to what they have grasped by faith."	The liturgy in its turn moves the faithful, filled with "the paschal sacraments," to be "one in holiness"; it prays that "they may hold fast in their lives to what they have grasped by their faith"; the renewal in the Eucharist of the covenant between the Lord and man draws the faithful into the compelling love of Christ and sets them on fire. *Sacrosanctum Concilium* (10)	Eucharistic
	This is especially true of the Liturgy of the Word in the celebration of Mass, in which the proclaiming of the death and resurrection of Christ is inseparably joined to the response of the people who hear, and to the very offering whereby Christ ratified the New Testament in blood. Pope Paul VI, *Presbyterorum Ordinis* (4)	Eucharistic
From this living explanation, the word of God proclaimed in the readings and the Church's celebration of the day's Liturgy will have greater impact. But this demands that the homily be truly the fruit of meditation, carefully prepared, neither too long nor too short... (24)	Much attention must be given to the homily: it should be neither too long nor too short; it should always be carefully prepared, rich in substance. Pope John Paul II, *Catechesi Tradendae* (48)	Prepared
... and suited to all those present, even children and the uneducated. (24)	Adapted to the hearers, and reserved to ordained ministers. Pope John Paul II, *Catechesi Tradendae* (48)	Adapted

This concise schema of preaching goes a long way to carve out the preaching task in modern times, and particularly in what the popes beginning with John Paul II call the New Evangelization. Pope John Paul described the kind of preaching he was looking for as "proclaimed with authority," "preached with conviction" and, significantly, "never watered down to make it more palatable": in other words, uncompromising (*Apostolorum Successores*, 121). In that same document directed to bishops, he calls for preaching that is

> imbued with pastoral charity

> developed in an appropriate style

> inspired by the great masters, especially the Fathers of the Church. (121)

He clarifies all this by insisting that preaching be

> presented attractively, as doctrine not only preached, but also practised

> anchored in the doctrine of the Church

> rooted in scripture. (121)

Stressing the re-visioning of the homily called for in the council, Pope John Paul underlines that the homily is "an integral part of the liturgy" and "the sum of all forms of preaching" (122). Thus, the preaching must

> present Catholic truth in its fullness

> use simple, familiar language suited to the listeners

> focus on the texts of the day's liturgy. (122)

Such preaching is, then, faithful to the Church's agenda, not the preacher's. It takes care to communicate that truth to listeners in ways that will help them understand and appropriate it. Significantly, it is not just scripturally based, but based firmly on the scriptures of the day's liturgy – the scriptures that the people have just heard as opposed to other scriptural references not heard that day. Such a view of preaching recaptures it as a primarily oral event – preaching that is heard in accessible language that declare that the scriptures just proclaimed are indeed fulfilled in the hearing of the listeners.

Pope Benedict XVI

Sacramentum Caritatis was the first post-synodal apostolic exhortation in Pope Benedict's pontificate. This pope devotes a section to the homily, opening with an understatement: "Given the importance of the word of God, the quality of homilies needs to be improved" (46). It was to become repeated many times. This document begins to lay out Pope Benedict's take on the homily based completely on the renewal of preaching in the council. He states that preaching is "part of the liturgical action" and "is meant to foster a deeper understanding of the Word of God so that it can bear fruit in the lives of the faithful" (46). He turns to preachers with advice on how to accomplish this. He asks that ordained ministers

- prepare the homily carefully
- develop a sufficient knowledge of scripture
- avoid generic and abstract preaching
- relate the Word of God to the sacramental celebration
- relate the Word of God to the life of the community. (46)

While not ruling out the thematic homily, he clearly relegates it to an occasional practice requiring prudence. While noting that catechesis and paraenesis "should not be forgotten," they are an extension and support for the primary focus on the Word of God that preachers are to apply in concrete, rather than abstract, ways to the sacrament of that liturgy and to the lived experience of the listener. Again, preaching is to be liturgical, conversational, scriptural and prophetic.

This pope repeats this vision in *Verbum Domini*, the 2010 post-synodal apostolic exhortation that followed the synod on the Word of God in the Life and Mission of the Church. He also expands upon it. If preaching the Word is meant to bear fruit in the lives of the faithful, it is to do so in the following way: "The homily is a means of bringing the scriptural message to life in a way that helps the faithful to realize that God's word is present and at work in their everyday lives" (59). Mary Catherine Hilkert O.P. calls this "naming grace" and argues that it is a fundamental defining aspect of Catholic preaching – a preaching she says is formed by a sacramental imagination (*Naming Grace*, 48).

Preachers name the grace that is at work even in the most difficult situations. They uncover the grace at work even while naming the darkness. It is modelled on the message of the cross that in the midst of the worst of things, God is at work making the best of things.

The pope also clarifies his call for relating the Word to both the sacramental celebration and the life of the community. *Verbum Domini* says that the homily "should lead to an understanding of the mystery being celebrated, serve as a summons to mission, and prepare the assembly for the profession of faith, the universal prayer and the Eucharistic liturgy" (59). While *Sacramentum Caritas* tells preachers to avoid the generic and the abstract, *Verbum Domini* tells us why: "Generic and abstract homilies which obscure the directness of God's word should be avoided, as well as useless digressions which risk drawing greater attention to preachers than to the heart of the Gospel message" (59). Thus, Pope Benedict is asking his preachers for a direct word that points not to preachers and their own learning, experience or agenda, but to Christ and his Gospel. A particularly beautiful sentence brings together what at first glance seems to be two contradictory principles: that it is personal and at the same time Christocentric. "The faithful should be able to perceive clearly that the preacher has a compelling desire to present Christ, who must stand at the center of every homily" (59). Preachers are, the pope continues, "to preach with conviction and passion" (59). The homily is personal because it is passionate. The compelling desire of preachers must be evident to the assembly. John Wesley's famous quote expresses this personal aspect of preaching: "I set myself on fire and people come to watch me burn." The American bishops called this view of preaching "a person of faith speaking" (*Fulfilled in Your Hearing*, 15). Preachers are personally invested in the homily, yet the homily points not to them, but to Christ. The homily is personal in that the personal commitment and faith of preachers animates the message, giving it a voice, language and imagery for the listeners in a liturgical setting who are also people of faith.

Verbum Domini presents a homily preparation method intended to make preaching both personal and Christocentric. It asks preachers to spend significant time meditating and praying over the text guided by three essential questions:

1. What are the scriptures being proclaimed in that liturgy saying?

2. What do they say to preachers personally?

3. What should preachers say to the specific community in its particular situation?

These questions keep preachers focused on the scriptures that the listeners hear. The questions direct preachers to an interior examination of how they relate to their own lived experience which, while not necessarily or even desirably made explicit in the homily, becomes a foundation for preachers to understand the texts and plumb their depths. Finally, they guide preachers to bring all this to bear in concrete ways to the specific needs and experience of the people to whom they are preaching. Thus, there is no question of preachers using a canned homily, something lifted from a website or other source. It must be the interpretive product of the preacher's experience directly referenced to the experience and needs of a specific assembly in a specific place in the context of the Church and from the scriptures.

Although understated in his "the quality of homilies needs to be improved," writing as Cardinal Ratzinger, Pope Benedict was somewhat more forceful.

> The crisis in Christian preaching, which we have experienced in growing proportions for a century, is based in no small part on the fact that the Christian answers have ignored man's questions: they remain right, but because they were not developed from and within the question, they remain ineffective. (Der Heutige Mensch vor der Gottesfrage, in *Dogma and Preaching*, 77)

The call to improve preaching actually comes from an assessment of modern preaching being in crisis. That crisis can be traced, according to the future pope, to a neglect of the listeners, their needs and, in particular, their questions. If preachers give the right answers to questions no one is really asking, and ignore the questions on the front burner, this pope says preachers are "ineffective." Guerric Debona, OSB, in his fine book *Preaching Effectively, Revitalizing Your Church*, gives a graphic example of this. Commenting on the churches filled to overflowing after the destruction of the World Trade Center on September 11, 2001, he notes that although some churches addressed it, there were far more churches of every denomination who did not even acknowledge that the Tuesday before had been in any way different. That was a fatal flaw in preaching to the Christian assembly. Undoubtedly, members of the frightened congregation attending worship the weekend following 9/11 had images burned in their head: of people jumping off the Twin Towers, or the smoke and the rubble of Ground Zero flooding the streets of lower Manhattan, of people in despair and confusion. (27)

They had come with questions, but in the language of Pope Benedict, heard instead valid answers to other questions they were not asking at that moment; as a result, church attendance went down in the following weeks. The answer to their questions can be found only in Christ, which is why Cardinal Ratzinger insisted on Christocentric preaching to accomplish what he saw was the goal of preaching. That goal is simply "for a man to say Yes to the offer of God's love that he encounters in Christ" (Christozentrik in der Verkundigung in *Dogma and Preaching*, 53). Christ, not doctrines, is the centre of preaching for Pope Benedict.

> Christian preaching is not the proclamation of a system of doctrines that follow from one another, but rather guidance to a reality that is challenge, gift and promise all in one. ... This means, furthermore, that Christian preaching is never purely doctrinal; rather, it has a Sitz im Leben, and the sociological setting with which it must stay in touch if it is not to die out, is the liturgy. (Christozentrik in der Verkundigung in *Dogma and Preaching*, 47)

Pope Francis

Pope Francis exemplifies all that the renewal of Catholic preaching envisioned. He models in his own practice what he asks of his preachers. His daily preaching in the intimate chapel at Domus Santae Marthae (St. Martha's House), where he has stayed since his installation as pope, is at once conversational, scriptural, prophetic and liturgical. It is also deeply pastoral. His main focus is first to proclaim the saving love of Christ so people can respond with the "Yes" that Pope Benedict insisted was the goal of preaching. In the much-discussed interview with Antonio Spadaro, editor-in-chief of *La Civiltà Cattolica,* in August 2013, Pope

Francis spoke about the need for a homily to be beautiful, and where that beauty comes from.

> I say this also thinking about the preaching and content of our preaching. A beautiful homily, a genuine sermon must begin with the first proclamation, the proclamation of salvation. There is nothing more solid, deep and sure than this proclamation. Then you have to do catechesis. Then you can draw even a moral consequence. But the proclamation of the saving love of God comes before moral and religious imperatives. Today sometimes it seems that the opposite order is prevailing.

Like Pope Benedict and Pope John Paul II before him, Pope Francis places neither moralism nor catechesis front and centre, nor does he rule them out. They come after the proclamation of what God has done first and serve to clarify that message and invitation to the listener. The listener, again, is key to this view of the homily.

> The homily is the touchstone to measure the pastor's proximity and ability to meet his people because those who preach must recognize the heart of their community and must be able to see where the desire of God is lively and ardent. The message of the Gospel, therefore, is not to be reduced to some aspects that although relevant, on their own do not show the heart of the message of Jesus Christ. (Spadaro)

It is in the extraordinary document *Evangelii Gaudium*, however, that Pope Francis most clearly states his vision of the homily. *Evangelii Gaudium* was issued in 2013 as the apostolic exhortation following the synod on the new evangelization. Significantly, one of the interventions at that synod identified preaching with evangelization. Bishop Senkiv stated, "Evangelization is the preaching of the word, which is the Word heard from God, and therefore it is a divine-human reality expressed in the form of an interpersonal dialogue" (October 15, 2012). It is not surprising, then, that the pope addresses the homily in this document. What is surprising is the amount of space he gives it. He devotes a hefty 24 sections to the homily and its preparation. Whereas Pope Benedict uses the carefully measured phrase "the quality of homilies needs to be improved," Pope Francis is somewhat – and characteristically – more direct.

We know that the faithful attach great importance to it, and that both they and their ordained ministers suffer because of homilies: the laity from having to listen to them and the clergy from having to preach them. (135)

Considering that poor preaching is, according to this pope, not simply ineffective but also painful, the pope insists that this "calls for serious consideration by pastors" (135). It is significant that he chooses to quote from Pope John Paul II in framing his description of what the Church is looking for from its preachers.

It is worth remembering that "the liturgical proclamation of the word of God, especially in the Eucharistic assembly, is not so much a time for meditation and catechesis as a dialogue between God and his people, a dialogue in which the great deeds of salvation are proclaimed and the demands of the covenant are continually restated." (137)

He presents a consistent line of thinking from the previous popes that informs his own concept of the homily. The homily is not to be used in either a highly personal way to expound on the preacher's own meditation or as a part of a catechetical program. Both meditation and catechesis must serve a much greater purpose, bringing the assembly and God together in a moment of grace-filled dialogue. Preachers bring forward the needs, concerns and questions of the people and bring to those questions the voice of God speaking through the Word at that liturgy. That requires a clear view of what preachers are doing. The pope observes that the homily has special characteristics because "it is a distinctive genre, since it is preaching situated within the framework of a liturgical celebration…" (137). Pope Francis elucidates those special characteristics in the following sections of *Evangelii Gaudium*.

Characteristics of the Homily

Preachers must know the heart of his community.	Section 137
The homily cannot be a form of entertainment.	Section 138
It should be brief.	Section 138

→

It should avoid taking on the semblance of a speech or a lecture.	Section 138
It is part of the offering made to the Father, and a mediation of the grace which Christ pours out during the celebration.	Section 138
Preaching should guide the assembly, and preachers, to a life-changing communion with Christ in the Eucharist.	Section 138
The Lord, more than his minister, will be the center of attention.	Section 138

Thus, as the renewal of the homily has called for since the Second Vatican Council, this pope describes a homily that is at once liturgical because it is part of the offering poured out in the celebration and which guides the listener and preacher to an encounter with Christ in the Eucharist, and is also focused on the listeners, not as a lecture, but as a dialogue facilitated by a preacher who knows their hearts.

To accomplish this both exalted and intimate view of preaching, the homily requires much from preachers. Above all, it requires commitment expressed in the dedication of significant time to homily preparation. "Preparation for preaching is so important a task that a prolonged time of study, prayer, reflection and pastoral creativity should be devoted to it" (145). The pope does not mince words about this. So pastoral and gentle in his address to lay people, this pontiff can be severe when addressing his clerics as to their responsibilities in fulfilling their vocations.

> Some pastors argue that such preparation is not possible given the vast number of tasks which they must perform; nonetheless, I presume to ask that each week a sufficient portion of personal and community time be dedicated to this task, even if less time has to be given to other important activities. Trust in the Holy Spirit who is at work during the homily is not merely passive but active and creative. It demands that we offer ourselves and all our abilities as instruments (cf. *Rom* 12:1) which God can use. A preacher who does not prepare is not "spiritual"; he is dishonest and irresponsible with the gifts he has received. (145)

A reader might be tempted to say "them's fightin' words," but the pope draws out the implication of preaching being the primary apostolate in terms of what it means for clergy investing themselves in homily preparation. It is also significant that the pope mentions not just personal time, but community time devoted to this preparation. That will come into play in a discussion of preparation methods later in this book.

Preachers will find it useful to clarify what they are doing in the pulpit by examining their own image for preaching. Fr. Robert Waznak explores the traditional images of preaching in *Introduction to the Homily*:

The Herald	This image is identified in the ordination rite for deacons. "Receive the Gospel whose herald you now are. Believe what you read, teach what you believe, practice what you teach." Preachers identifying with this image proclaim the kerygma – the Good News – announcing it to the people.
The Teacher	Preachers identifying predominantly with this image see themselves as primarily explaining and teaching the truths of the faith. For them, the catechetical and instructional aspect of the homily is most pronounced.
The Interpreter	Preachers who see themselves as interpreters tend to use story and image as they bring the contemporary situation into focus through the interpretive lens of scripture.
The Witness	Witness preachers stand in the pulpit primarily as a person of faith speaking to people of faith. While not necessarily speaking of their own experience explicitly, their personal encounter with Christ is expressed in a commitment and urgency that what they have to say touches them personally and is urgent.

Other writers have added different images, including the Storyteller and the Pastor. Pope Francis, in *Evangelii Gaudium*, offers his own image for consideration. It is an image that clearly governs his own preaching and an image that he recommends to his preachers. Writing about the Church as the people of God constantly evangelizing itself, he adds:

> It reminds us that the Church is a mother, and that she preaches in the same way that a mother speaks to her child, knowing that the child trusts that which she is teaching is for his or her benefit, for children know that they are loved. Moreover, a good mother can recognize everything that God is bringing about in her children, she listens to their concerns and learns from them. (139)

The image of preacher as a mother talking to her children who know that they are loved suggests an approach that is intimate, loving and concerned for their well-being, and that establishes trust. The teaching proceeds from this foundation. It is, Francis says, a preaching that is heart-to-heart, which refers to Cardinal Newman's motto: *cor ad cor loquitur*. That intimate quality is important to this pope before all else. "Preachers have the wonderful but difficult task of joining loving hearts, the hearts of the Lord and his people" (143). That has much to do with the content of the homily.

> A preaching which would be purely moralistic or doctrinaire, or one which turns into a lecture on biblical exegesis, detracts from this heart-to-heart communication which takes place in the homily and possesses a quasi-sacramental character. (142)

How does a preacher accomplish this kind of preaching? *Evangelii Gaudium* lays out a preparation plan for preachers to reach these goals.

Preaching Plan

Call upon the Holy Spirit.	Section 146
Give full attention to the biblical texts of that liturgy which are to be the basis of the preaching.	Section 146
Discover the principal message that the author intended.	Section 147
Identify the effects that the author wanted to produce.	Section 147

Relate the central message to the teaching of the entire Bible as handed on by the Church.	Section 148
In the presence of God, during a recollected reading of the text, ask: Lord, what does this text say to me?	Section 153
Keep an ear close to the people to discover what the faithful needs to hear.	Section 154
Link the message of the biblical text to a human situation, to an experience which cries out for the light of God's word.	Section 154

The Pope proposes that preachers uses *Lectio Divina* for a slow, recollected reading of the scriptures of that liturgy. He also insists that preachers respect the text by starting with and giving sufficient time to the literal meaning rather than what preachers would like the scripture to mean.

> The spiritual reading of a text must start with its literal sense. Otherwise we can easily make the text say what we think is convenient, useful for confirming us in our previous decisions, suited to our own patterns of thought. Ultimately, this would be tantamount to using something sacred for our own benefit and then passing on this confusion to God's people. We must never forget that sometimes "even Satan disguises himself as an angel of light" (2 Cor 11:14). (152)

Meditating on the scriptures of that liturgy and situating them in the context of the whole of scripture and Church teaching is essential in the process of bringing them to bear on contemporary life. At the same time, the pope is careful to caution:

> It does not mean that we can weaken the distinct and specific emphasis of a text which we are called to preach. One of the defects of a tedious and ineffectual preaching is precisely its inability to transmit the intrinsic power of the text which has been proclaimed. (148)

In this way, the pope traces poor preaching, preaching that is "tedious and ineffectual," to a failure to emphasize the text of that liturgy and to bring out the power of the Word that is in that text.

Bringing that text to bear on contemporary life requires humility. It is not an occasion for preachers to substitute a personal agenda, a personal take on world events, for the homily.

> Let us also keep in mind that we should never respond to questions that nobody asks. Nor is it fitting to talk about the latest news in order to awaken people's interest; we have television programmes for that. It is possible, however, to start with some fact or story so that God's word can forcefully resound in its calls to conversion, worship, commitment to fraternity and service, and so forth. Yet there will always be some who readily listen to a preacher's commentaries on current affairs, while not letting themselves be challenged. (155)

The caveat against answering unasked questions echoes Pope Benedict's indictment of the crisis of preaching arising from right answers to questions no one is posing. Pope Francis clarifies that bringing scripture as a lens on contemporary lived experience does not mean turning the homily into a news commentary driven by the agenda of preachers. The goal remains of bringing scripture to bear on the listeners' lives so they can better enter into conversion and worship, or as Pope Benedict puts it, to say "yes" to God, and to open their hearts for service to others.

Having outlined what he sees a homily is, and what a preacher is to do in preparation, Pope Francis then turns to delivery. He tells his preachers that the way a homily is delivered is not to be an afterthought.

> Some people think they can be good preachers because they know what ought to be said, but pay no attention to how it should be said, that is, the concrete way of constructing a sermon. They complain when people do not listen to or appreciate them, but perhaps they have never taken the trouble to find the proper way of presenting their message. (156)

Rather than blaming the listeners for limited attention spans or an unwillingness to work at understanding the homily, preachers are called to look at what they themselves do. To do so is an act of charity, says the pope, and indicates the humility of preachers.

Concern for the way we preach is likewise a profoundly spiritual concern. It entails responding to the love of God by putting all our talents and creativity at the service of the mission which he has given us; at the same time, it shows a fine, active love of neighbor by refusing to offer others a product of poor quality. (156)

Refusing to deliver a poor homily means paying attention to the dynamics of speaking: volume, voice colour, rate of speech, eye contact and gestures. It means, the pope emphasizes, using simple, understandable language that is adapted to the listeners. It means being concerned for clarity by delivering an organized, cohesive homily. In particular, it means that the homily has thematic unity, that is, it is centred on a single point worth making and which can be easily grasped (158). One of the most important ways to ensure unity and to express that unity in clear, understandable ways adapted to the listener is through preferring images to examples.

Sometimes examples are used to clarify a certain point, but these examples usually appeal only to the mind; images, on the other hand, help people better appreciate and accept the message we wish to communicate. An attractive image makes the message seem familiar, close to home, practical and related to everyday life. A successful image can make people savour the message, awaken a desire and move the will towards the Gospel. (157)

Pope Francis takes great care to follow his own advice in his preaching, whether it be his homilies at special liturgies during Holy Week or his daily preaching at the chapel in Domus Sanctae Marthae where he lives.

The Homiletic Directory

The Homiletic Directory is a precious jewel that began under the pontificate of Benedict XVI and that the Church presented to its clergy under Pope Francis. It was a request from the Fathers of the Synod on the Word of God in the Life of the Church. In the third General Congregation, H.E. Most Rev. Mark Benedict Coleridge, Archbishop of Canberra-Goulburn, Australia, stated:

The Second Vatican Council call for a renewal of preaching involved a shift from the sermon understood primarily as an exposition of Catholic doctrine, devotion and discipline to the homily understood primarily as an exposition and application of Scripture. Such a shift has been accomplished only in part. One reason for this is that preaching too often takes the kerygma for granted, and this at a moment in Western cultures when the kerygma cannot be taken for granted. If it is, there is the risk of a moralistic reduction of preaching which make evoke interest or admiration but not the faith that saves. Preaching will not be an experience of Christ's power. (Tuesday, 7 October 2008 – Morning)

Cardinal Coleridge proposed help for the Church's preachers in the form of a homiletic guide.

A new evangelization requires a new formulation and proclamation of the kerygma in the interests of a more powerful missionary preaching. To promote such a preaching a General Homiletic Directory could be prepared along the lines of the General Catechetical Directory and the General Instruction of the Roman Missal. (Tuesday, 7 October 2008 – Morning)

Such a directory, he continued, would articulate what the Church asks from its preachers and give them the tools to accomplish it. He was careful to stress that such a directory was meant to help, not be a straitjacket, so that the individual gifts of preachers and the particular situation of the preaching situation would be taken into account.

Such a directory would draw upon the experience of the universal Church in providing a framework without stifling the genius of particular Churches or individual preachers. It would help to ensure a more solid and systematic preparation for preachers in seminaries and houses of formation, and this at a time when all recognize how vital preaching is, since the one point of contact with the Word of God for most Catholic people is the celebration of the Sunday Eucharist with its homily. (Tuesday, 7 October 2008 – Morning)

What Cardinal Coleridge proposed as a "could" became a request from Pope Benedict XVI two years later in *Verbum Domini*:

I ask the competent authorities, along the lines of the Eucharistic Compendium, also to prepare practical publications to assist ministers in carrying out their task as best they can: as for example a Directory on the homily, in which preachers can find useful assistance in preparing to exercise their ministry. (60)

Two years after that, the Fathers of the Congregation for Divine Worship and the Discipline of the Sacraments approved a draft of the Homiletic Directory in two sessions on February 7 and May 20, 2014. Cardinal Llovera, prefect of the dicastery, signed it on June 29 and it was published on February 10, 2015. The Directory makes it clear that it is the fruit of the renewal of the homily building upon the marvellous work that preceded it. It notes that the Directory is based on *Sacrosanctum Concilium* from the Council; *The Introduction to the Lectionary of the Mass*, which incorporates the thinking of Paul VI and John Paul II; *The General Instruction of the Roman Missal*; Benedict XVI's *Sacramentum Caritatis* and *Verbum Domini*; and Francis' *Evangelii Gaudium*.

The first part of the Directory, "The Homily and Its Liturgical Setting," presents a theology of the homily that declares first what the homily is and what it is not. The second part, *Ars Praedicandi*, presents interpretive keys for each Sunday and feast of each liturgical year. Two appendices follow that section. The first presents references to the *Catechism of the Catholic Church* that bear upon the readings for each Sunday. The second outlines a helpful list of Vatican documents on the homily that have been published since the council.

The Directory marks a change in preaching from "a moral or doctrinal instruction delivered at Mass on Sundays and holy days, not necessarily integrated into the celebration itself" (1), describing what the homily is called to be now, and what it is not to be.

The Homily Is

1. Variable

It is variable in that the homily is not a one-size-fits-all venture. The homily responds to what the Directory calls "cultural differences and the gifts of preachers." Culture does mean ethnicity, but it is also far more than that. Parishes within the same country can have their own cultures. The culture of a rural parish will be different from a city parish, and Masses within a parish also develop their own culture, with a particular constituency with even its own style of music. Thus, the homily needs to be adapted. What does that culture need to hear, and what are the language, images and methods most suited to them? Finally, what are the natural gifts of preachers and how do they fit in?

2. An integral part of the liturgy

The homily is not a pause in the celebration. Neither is it something that has its own beginning and conclusion, as if a separate entity. It functions as a part of a whole. The Directory advises preachers to use both the biblical passages and the prayers of the liturgical celebration. These prayers, it urges, should not be overlooked because the collect, the responsorial psalm, the Gospel acclamation, the prayer after Communion – indeed all the prayers said in the Mass – "provide a useful hermeneutic for the preacher's interpretation of the biblical texts" (11). The homily stitches these parts together to make the unity of the Mass explicit. Thus, "what distinguishes a homily from other forms of instruction is its liturgical context" (11).

3. An act of worship

One consequence of understanding the homily as integrated with the liturgy is to see it not primarily as a teaching tool, but as part of the Mass – an act of worship. The Directory explains this further by calling the homily a "hymn of gratitude for the magnolia Dei that tells the assembled that God's Word is fulfilled in their hearing, but praises God for this fulfillment" (4).

4. Sacramental

In a significant reference to Pope Paul VI, the Homiletic Directory echoes the words of *Mysterium Fidei*, declaring that "Christ is present in the assembly gathered to listen to his word and in the preaching of his minister, through whom the same Lord who spoke long ago in the synagogue of Nazareth now instructs his people" (4). This sacramental presence of Christ explains why the Directory maintains the Church's insistence that the faculty to preach is not simply based on ability, but rather on a calling through ordination. Consequently, it upholds that the homily is to be delivered "only by bishops, priests, or deacons" (40). The homily envisages that although ordinarily it is the presider who should preach at the Mass, other priests and deacons are called to preach as well. In other words, the homily is preached "always by one ordained to preside or assist at the altar" (5).

5. Tailored

Just as the homily is variable according to the gifts of preachers and the culture in which it is preached, it is also specifically tailored. The Directory advises preachers to make the assembly their inspiration for preaching. This is another way of saying that preachers need to attend to an exegesis of assembly. The Directory notes, "it should also be emphasized that the homily should be tailored to the needs of the particular community, and indeed draw inspiration from it" (8). This is not to give the community what it wants, what will please, but gives them what they need to hear, what bears upon their lives, in a way that will most make sense to them.

The Homily Is Not

1. Abstract

A constant theme in the writings of the recent popes on homiletics is that preachers should avoid remaining on an elevated, abstract level of general concepts and theological terms. The homily is not meant to be a watered-down theology class. Rather, preachers are meant to prefer the concrete through specific image, example and application to the contemporary in precise and evocative language.

2. Unrelated to the readings

The Directory calls preachers to avoid misusing the readings of the Mass for their own agendas. The focus is meant to be on a faithful interpretation of the readings of the day. It cautions, "the Mass is not an occasion for the preacher to address some issue completely unrelated to the liturgical celebration and its readings, or to do violence to the texts provided by the Church by twisting them to fit some pre-conceived idea" (6). That is, preachers are not to hijack the Mass and inflict their views upon a captive assembly. To avoid that, preachers need to see the interconnectedness of the prayers and readings of the liturgy as a "constellation" (16) that they interpret within the living tradition of the Church and the analogy of faith (17).

3. An exercise in exegesis

Although preachers are to keep the homily focused on scripture, it is not to turn the homily into a Bible study. The Directory observes that even if this were desirable, there is simply not the time to do this well (6). This is closely connected to the next point.

4. Catechetical instruction

Like exegesis, catechesis may be an element in the homily, but it is not to *be* the homily. The Directory clarifies this point: "As with biblical exegesis, there is not the time to do this properly; furthermore, this would represent a variation on the practice of presenting a discourse at Mass that is not really integral to the liturgical celebration itself" (6).

5. A personal witness

Some preachers may find this caveat against personal witness surprising, or even troubling. As with exegesis and catechesis, personal witness can be an element that serves the message, the proclamation of the kerygma and the purpose of the homily as praise. The warning here is to not allow personal witness to eclipse the rest and become the homily. The Directory notes: "Finally, the time for the homily should not be taken up with the preacher's personal witness. There is no question that people can be deeply moved by personal stories, but the homily should express the faith of the Church, and simply the preacher's story" (6). Thus, self-references should be few and far between – and only made, if made at all, insofar as the self-reference actually points to Christ. That it should not be a personal witness does not mean that the homily should not be personal, however. The Directory is careful to point out that the person of the preacher is meant to come through in the preaching. "Furthermore, the preacher needs to speak in such a way that his hearers can sense his belief in the power of God" (7).

Having clearly delineated what the homily is not, the Directory adds an important qualification:

> In saying that the homily is none of these things, this does not mean that topical themes, biblical exegesis, doctrinal instruction, and personal witness have no place in preaching: indeed, they can be effective as elements in a good homily. ... Like fire, all of these things make good servants but poor masters: if they serve the purpose of the homily, they are good; if they take the place of the homily, they are not. (7)

With this understanding of what to do and not to do in the homily, preachers using the Directory look at the organization and development of the homily as a sequence of movements.

Movement 1

The homily grows out of the readings, interprets them in the light of the death and resurrection of Christ and uses them as an interpretive lens for the contemporary experience of the listeners.

Movement 2

Preachers then prepare the community to enter into and more fully appreciate the sacrament of that liturgy.

Movement 3

The last movement deals with how the listeners will live out the call of the Gospel, their own witness after the *Ite Missa Est* in their homes, communities and workplaces. The Directory is careful to point out, however, that this final section should be very brief – and should still highlight the grace in the sacrament that makes their witness possible. That is, speaking about what *the listeners* do should not eclipse the primary focus of what *God* has done, is doing and will do.

The Directory advises that developing a homily with these three movements requires both prayer and study (26) – but underlines that while study is "invaluable," prayer is "essential." Consequently, it advises preachers to use *Lectio Divina* as their spiritual practice to prepare for their preaching. The steps it describes are well known:

Lectio	discerning what the texts say in themselves
Meditatio	discerning what the texts say to the preacher personally and to the community
Oratio	responding to God after hearing his voice in his Word
Contemplatio	determining what conversion is called for in response to the Word

To this list, the Directory adds one more step from Pope Benedict XVI:

Actio	determining the action that the believer is called to take for others.

From there, preachers can turn to study. Just as they have their own favourite resources, this directory offers itself as a trusted resource, a compass to help them stay on track. Thus, the themes in *Ars Praedicandi* and the references to the *Catechism of the Catholic Church* are meant to be helpful, not prescriptive. At the same time, preachers should not treat the Directory as one-stop shopping – going only to this resource or going there in advance of prayer and meditation to find out a theme or a reference. It will be a precious jewel in homiletic preparation when incorporated into a committed and prayerful process of listening to the Word, the Church and the assembly.

Part 2

What Makes for Good Catholic Preaching?

All the popes since the Second Vatican Council have stressed that preachers need to take preaching seriously, make it a priority and, above all, spend significant time on it. The question is, even if preachers do these things, how do they know that they are on the right track – that they are accomplishing what the Church wants from them? Having a clear picture of what good Catholic preaching looks like before embarking on it helps clarify the target at which preachers are aiming, and at the same time gives them some yardsticks, some measuring points, against which to evaluate how well they have done. With these marks firmly grasped, preachers can then consider how to achieve them in practical terms. These marks can be expressed in several ways.

The four marks of preaching

The Nicene Creed professes that the Church has four marks. It is at once "one, holy, catholic and apostolic." The *Catechism of the Catholic Church* tells us that these four marks are the "deepest and ultimate identity" of the Church (865). The Church has also designated four marks of preaching that are the deepest and ultimate identity of preaching in modern times. Those marks, as seen in Part 1, are scriptural, liturgical, prophetic and conversational. They are the primary fruit of the homiletic renewal in the last half-century and represent a reset in the calling of preaching to meet the needs of the listener in the service of the Church.

Scriptural

A scriptural homily is primarily concerned with the scriptures heard in that liturgy. The homily is based on them and is an extension of them. Rather than avoiding them, or using them as a springboard to speak about something else, preachers take hold of the scriptures heard and let them drive the homily. A scriptural homily respects the literal sense of the text rather than making scripture say what the preacher or listener would like it to say. At the same time, it opens up the spiritual meaning of the text to the listener.

Liturgical

Before the council, it was possible to hold the following view of the homily:

> Preaching the Word of God holds an honored place in the liturgy of the Church, not as part of it, but as a supplement to it. (Harrahan, "Must We Have Sermons?" *Homiletics and Pastoral Review* 47 [1947], 333)

This is no longer the case. The Church has called for a different view of the homily in modern times. The popes have consistently emphasized that the homily is part of the liturgy, not extraneous to it or a supplementary component. As integral to the liturgy, the homily is also praise and prayer – and a grace-filled moment for encountering God. Fr. Michael Monshau, OP writes that this approach to preaching comes from the restoration of the Word in the liturgy.

> The 20th-century restoration has reclaimed for the contemporary Church a liturgical praxis that nourishes the faithful at two tables: the table of the Word and the table of the Eucharist. Hence, liturgy becomes a "Double Feast." (Monshau, *Preaching at the Double Feast*, Collegeville, MN: Liturgical Press, 2006, 1)

Understanding the homily in the context of a double feast has profound implications for preachers and gives their preaching a particularly Catholic identity.

A liturgical homily proceeds from all that went before it: the processional hymn, the collect, the penitential rite, the Gloria, the readings and the responsorial psalm. It does not need an introduction in the same way as a talk or speech might, because it is part of a grand movement for which the context has already been set. Preachers of liturgical homilies are fully aware of the liturgical context both of that particular liturgy and of the season, and thus make use of these references and connections. They also keep the sacrament of that liturgy prominent, encouraging and enabling a fuller participation in it.

Prophetic

Preachers preach prophetically when they take care to draw the connection between the scriptures proclaimed and the contemporary experience of the listeners. They preach in the present tense – that is, they preach not only what God did in scripture in the past, but what God is doing now. They preach what God said to his people then and what God speaks to his people now. In this way, preaching is, as Pope Benedict wrote as Cardinal Ratzinger, both synchronic and diachronic ("Church as the Place of Preaching" [Kirche als Ord der Verkundigun], in *Dogma and Preaching*, 24). Exegesis of the scriptures in the liturgy becomes combined with what writers like Fr. Guerric DeBona and others call "exegesis of congregation" (DeBona, *Preaching Effectively: Revitalizing Your Church*, 266). In this way, the preaching responds not to the questions that preachers pose, but rather to the questions and concerns of the listener.

Conversational

Conversational preaching connects with the listeners through language and images that are readily understandable. That language and those images will differ from place to place and from community to community. Conversational preachers, concerned about the clarity of their message, consider carefully if there are any obstacles to what they are preaching that might make it less accessible. Those obstacles might be unfamiliar vocabulary, references that the listeners do not know, images to which they cannot connect, or simply a tone that puts distance between them and the preacher. Conversational preachers are not primarily concerned with a polished text and getting the homily word perfect, as is done in putting together an essay. Rather, they want to get the idea of the homily perfect, using words that relate. They look for ways to relate the homily to the listeners and to make it memorable for them so they can reflect on it later.

Another approach: personal, liturgical, inculturated, clarifying and actualizing

Fr. Stephen Vincent DeLeers wrote an excellent account of the development of modern Catholic preaching in his 2004 book *Written Text Becomes Living Word*. He writes of Catholic preaching, "The homily is the act that, beyond all odds, allows an ancient text from a foreign culture to be received as God's Word today, relevant and powerful" (49). After examining what the Church has been asking for, he presents his own version of preaching outcomes, or marks of the homily: personal, liturgical, inculturated, clarifying and actualizing (PLICA). Let's look at each outcome separately.

Personal

St. Augustine argued in Book IV of *De Doctrina Christiana* (On Christian Doctrine) for appropriating classical rhetorical skills and putting them to use in preaching. Aristotle had posited *logos*, addressing the word to the mind; *pathos*, addressing the word to the heart or emotions; and *ethos*, the compelling integrity of the speaker. Augustine asserted that the person of the preacher coming through in the preaching was critical to its effectiveness. He wrote, "But whatever may be the majesty of the style, the life of the speaker will count for more in securing the hearer's compliance" (ch. 27). Cardinal Newman called this quality "earnestness." Preachers are called to convey to listeners earnestness, that sense of commitment to the message and its urgency. Newman described it this way:

> But, not to go to the consideration of divine influences, which is beyond my subject, the very presence of simple earnestness is even in itself a powerful natural instrument to affect that toward which it is directed. Earnestness creates earnestness in others by sympathy; and the more a preacher loses and is lost to himself, the more does he gain his brethren. Nor is it without some logical force also; for what is powerful enough to absorb and possess a preacher has at least a prima facie claim

of attention on the part of the hearers. (London: Basil Montagu Pickering, 1873, 407)

Such preaching is *personal* because the preacher is "all in." Newman gives this quality the strongest possible emphasis:

> On these grounds, I would go on to lay down a precept, which I trust is not extravagant, when allowance is made for the preciseness and the point which are unavoidable in all categorical statements upon matters of conduct. It is that preachers should neglect everything whatever besides devotion to their one object, and earnestness in pursuing it, till they in some good measure attain to these requisites. (408)

DeLeers also puts this quality in first place: "Before it is anything else, the Sunday homily is the word of a person of faith, the word of a person who has experienced the Lord and who wishes to share that experience" (53). This does not necessarily mean being self-referential, which carries the risk of drawing attention to the preacher rather than to Christ. A homily is not meant to lead the assembly to admire the preacher for what he has done or for his learning, nor sympathize or emphasize with him for the difficult struggles in his life. That would be to displace Christ as the centre, so that the assembly focuses on the signpost rather than on the destination. It does mean that being personal comes through, as DeLeers shows, in manifesting genuineness, faith and pastoral love. The American bishops wrote in *Fulfilled in Your Hearing* that what parishioners want most from the homilies is "simply a person of faith speaking" (15). That is, a person of faith speaks to a people of faith in what Pope Francis adds in *Evangelii Gaudium*: an intimate, heart-to-heart fashion.

> This setting, both maternal and ecclesial, in which the dialogue between the Lord and his people takes place, should be encouraged by the closeness of the preacher, the warmth of his tone of voice, the unpretentiousness of his manner of speaking, the joy of his gestures. Even if the homily at times may be somewhat tedious, if this maternal and ecclesial spirit is present, it will always bear fruit, just as the tedious counsels of a mother bear fruit, in due time, in the hearts of her children. (140)

In other words, the person of the preacher speaking as one person to another brings the message of the homily to the heart of the listener.

Liturgical

The Sunday homily has become obligatory ever since the Second Vatican Council. However, preaching that is *liturgical* means much more than just the obligation to preach. It also refers to an understanding of preaching as part of liturgy. Fr. DeLeers writes:

> For the homily is a part of the liturgy and so shares the nature of the liturgy: the homily, too, is an act of worship. The homilist, too, in word and gesture, must communicate a sense of the sacred. Two important means to this end are effective proclamation of Scripture and ritual presence. (71)

The popes have asserted that the homily is part of and integral to the liturgy, emphasizing its place in the celebration. DeLeers' treatment of preaching that is liturgical in the PLICA system gets at the how of preaching in order to recognize its place as part of unfolding liturgy. In terms of content, of what is said, a homily that is an act of worship in the liturgy can situate itself explicitly in the liturgical season, and in the sacrament of that celebration. In terms of delivery, how it is said, DeLeers describes a preaching that attends to effective proclamation of the Gospel and communicates a sense of the sacred in the preaching. It also has to do with what DeLeers describes as "a thoughtful and prayerful ritual presence – to space and assembly" that "predisposes our listeners to attend to our words as the words of a fellow worshipper of God" (72). Certainly, homilies are listened to through various media out of the context of liturgy, and they are published and read. The thing to keep in mind, a system like PLICA insists, is that although heard in these ways, this is not what they were primarily designed for. They are intentionally crafted and offered as an act of worship in the context of a liturgy of prayers, readings, music and responses, and so must reflect that context.

Inculturated

DeLeers adds *inculturated* to the list of qualities of outstanding preaching, but credits the incorporation of that term into Catholic teaching and into the conversation around homiletics to Pope John Paul II (88). Preaching that attends to inculturation looks to express the Gospel in ways that connect with peoples in different frames of reference. Cultures do not simply refer to ethnic backgrounds; many contexts and cultures exist within a society. Forms of expression that work for one do not necessarily work for another. DeLeers puts it this way: "The inculturating preacher's task is not only to speak plainly but also to clothe the gospel in the words and symbols of the gathered community" (91).

Thus, preachers make an effort to know their communities well in order to know what resonates and what sticks in people's memories. A homily that is effective for one community may not be right at all for another. What one community needs to hear at this time can be quite different from what another needs to hear – and the way they need to hear it also changes because of who they are, their culture.

Pope John Paul II gave inculturation a very high priority.

As she carries out missionary activity among the nations, the Church encounters different cultures and becomes involved in the process of inculturation. The need for such involvement has marked the Church's pilgrimage throughout her history, but today it is particularly urgent. (*Redemptoris Missio*, 52)

Clarifying

A clarifying homily brings things into focus. Preachers clarify what the texts actually mean, as opposed to an individual and unsubstantiated reading. They use a full range of both contemporary and traditional exegetical resources in their preparation. In addition to bringing these resources to the text, preachers also unpack the text in the context of Church teaching, shedding light on what the writer intended, what the listener of the time heard and what is being said to modern listeners. DeLeers extends this quality from a clear presentation of what the scriptures of that liturgy actually say to a focused single message for the homily– what Bishop Untener called "the pearl" or what celebrated homilist Thomas Long called a "focus statement."

Actualizing

An *actualizing* homily does not simply explain, clarify, exhort or instruct, as good as those things are. It goes beyond that. Something happens – something becomes present in a homily that actualizes the Word. DeLeers sets a high standard for this kind of preaching:

> The homily is no mere commentary on the Word but is itself a living word, capable of bearing the saving presence of Christ himself. The scriptural Word in itself is powerful, but the well-preached homily increases the efficacy of the Word. (119)

This exalted understanding of preaching grows from Pope Paul VI's view that Christ is present in preaching (*Mysterium Fidei*, 36). Listeners who hear such preaching do more than take in information; they have an encounter with Christ. DeLeers' model for this is the event on the road to Emmaus. After hearing how the scriptures speak of Jesus, the disciples say, "Were not our hearts burning within us while he was talking to us on the road, while he was opening the scriptures to us?" (Luke 24:31-32). Preaching in this way requires not an academic or casual attitude, but a reverence that the preacher is walking on hallowed ground and is doing anointed work. DeLeers writes:

> As we open the Lectionary early in the week, we must make an act of faith that through his Spirit, Jesus can open the Scriptures to us and manifest himself to us. We preachers are perennially the disciples on the road to Emmaus, meeting the Risen One in the interpretation of Scripture. (125)

Preachers who aim to actualize their homilies intend that what they preach about is made present. If they preach reconciliation, they intend to see it. If they preach faith, they are looking for it. If they preach conversion, contrition, repentance or healing, they expect that the Word of God does not return void.

Roman Catholic Homiletic Preaching Competencies

The Catholic Association of Teachers of Homiletics (CATH) brings together professors of homiletics from across North America. In 2002, it published a useful document that surveyed and evaluated the teaching of homiletics in the United States. *The State of Homiletics in the Seminaries and Graduate Schools of Theology in the United States* is a gem. In addition to its valuable insights and thoughtful suggestions on pedagogy, it proposes a set of competencies for Catholic preaching. In educational parlance, these are outcomes preachers can use to self-evaluate or have others evaluate them. They build on the work of Fr. DeLeers, who was a president of CATH and one of the main writers of the document. Acknowledging the PLICA system as their foundation, these competencies offer a great deal of clarity because each is accompanied by a set of specific descriptors that tell preachers what achieving that competency looks like.

Roman Catholic Homiletic Preaching Competencies

Personal (ability to present self and message to others)

> - engages listener by means of verbal and non-verbal communications skills
> - takes responsibility for choices made regarding content of preaching
> - manifests genuineness
> - manifests empathetic understanding of listeners
> - manifests pastoral love

Liturgical (ability to speak and act as a minister of the liturgy)

> - communicates a sense of the sacred
> - identifies with listeners and speaks on behalf of the assembly
> - reinforces listeners' experience of themselves as Church
> - connects word, ritual and assembly
> - encourages lively and personal participation in liturgy

Interpretive (ability to correlate and interpret scripture and human experience)

> - uses language easily understood by listeners
> - uses relevant language
> - names current cultural realities (including negative realities)
> - interprets scripture in terms of today's world
> - interprets today's world in the light of scripture

Clarifying (ability to speak clearly and insightfully about the scriptures)

> makes a central point clearly
> makes a central point worth making, theologically and pastorally
> utilizes responsibly exegetical scholarship
> utilizes responsibly contemporary theology
> reflects the fullness of Catholic Tradition

Sacramental (ability to facilitate actualization of scriptures)

"Were not our hearts burning within us, when he … opened the scripture to us?" [Lk 24:32]

> communicates sense of importance in what is being said
> awakens wonder at the Good News
> conveys a sense of expectation of God's presence in preaching
> communicates lived truth
> enables an experience of the Good News

Structured as outcomes, the sub-points of each competency begin with an action verb describing what the homily needs to do. When the listeners can say, "Yes, the homily did that," preachers know they have successfully met that competency. The CATH list contains *personal, liturgical* and *clarifying* from the PLICA system. What DeLeers describes under inculturated, the CATH competencies combine with the prophetic aspect of preaching and name *interpretive*. That is, while holding up scripture as a lens to interpret contemporary life, it does so in the context of the shared experience of the community. DeLeers' actualizing becomes expressed as *sacramental*, stressing mystery, incarnation and encounter.

A rubric for Catholic preaching

Several writers and teachers of homiletics have developed rubrics as helpful tools to give language to and measure how well a preacher is doing. The following rubric is one way of identifying what preachers do well and where they could focus their attention to make their preaching even better. It makes use of what the Church has been asking of its preachers and breaks that into six marks of good preaching: being focused, scriptural, liturgical, prophetic, conversational and personal. Rubrics commonly use a scale of four descriptors to measure success.

This rubric describes successful achievement in the first box. That descriptor is the homily's aim. The following boxes describe what might be working well and what might need attention.

Rubrics for Homily Feedback				
Focus	The homily has a clear central point that is worth making for this assembly.	The homily has a central point that is worth making, but needs some clarification to be understood.	The homily has a central point that is not worth making for this assembly and/or needs much more clarity.	The homily has divergent messages and/or many points that obscure a clear focus and that are difficult to remember.
Scriptural	The homily is clearly rooted in and developed from the readings of the liturgy.	The homily is mostly rooted in the readings of the liturgy, but some digressions, stories or images seem unconnected.	The liturgy somewhat uses the readings of the liturgy, but moves away to introduce themes that do not arise from them.	The homily makes marginal or no use of the scriptures of that liturgy.
Liturgical	The homily is clearly a part of the liturgy through explicit connections with ritual, sacrament and the liturgical season.	The homily demonstrates some connection with the rest of the liturgy, the liturgical seasons and the sacrament.	The homily occasionally makes a connection with the liturgy and sacrament.	The homily does not demonstrate connection with liturgy, the liturgical season or the sacrament.

➜

Rubrics for Homily Feedback (continued)				
Prophetic	The homily clearly brings the scripture to the contemporary experience and questions of the listeners in a way that illuminates them.	The homily generally interprets contemporary experiences through scripture, but more clarification or concrete example is needed.	The homily somewhat or occasionally interprets the contemporary through the lens of scripture.	The homily does not bring the texts of the liturgy to the contemporary situation or questions of the listeners.
Conversational	The homily is clearly expressed in language, image, story or other means readily grasped by the listener.	The homily is generally expressed conversationally aside from some word choices or examples that are not readily grasped by the intended listener.	The homily is somewhat conversational, but word choices, sentence structure, level of formality, examples, images or stories could be better adjusted for the listener.	The homily does not use language, sentence structure, level of formality, examples, images or stories adjusted for the listener.
Personal	The homily is delivered with conviction and confidence with good eye contact as one person speaking to another.	The homily is generally delivered with conviction and confidence as one person speaking to another.	The homily is somewhat delivered personally, but sometimes seems distant, dry or disconnected.	The homily needs to demonstrate conviction, and more personal connection with the listener.

A Personal Rubric for Preaching

Getting Feedback

Preachers have their own particular strengths that come naturally with their personalities. They have different gifts that relate to the different marks of good preaching. Some homilists are gifted in certain areas and require very little development, while other preachers find those areas challenging. Once preachers are clear on what the Church is asking of them, they do well to engage listeners for feedback. Yet very few Catholic preachers actually do this.

Dr. Lori Carrel's profile of preachers in *The Great American Sermon Survey* (2000) noted of both Catholic and Protestant preachers that "it is extremely rare for a preacher to have a formal process for soliciting input or instigating dialogue before, during or after the sermon" (123). Dr. Karla Bellinger also notes in her work how few preachers have any concrete idea of the impact their preaching actually has (8). Surveys of preachers and deacons conducted in Canada bear this out. The majority of preachers report that the only feedback they get is unsolicited as they stand in the vestibule of the church as the assembly leaves. Typically, that is "Good homily, Father/Deacon." Very few preachers attempt to get solicited feedback, yet this is the only way homilists can know if their central message gets through, if the homilies are clear and memorable, and if what they preach is connecting with the lives of the listeners. Preachers may think they have a focus, but how do they know for sure that the listeners hear that focus?

There are several ways of getting input, all of which make use of a clear understanding of the marks of good preaching.

1. Written Feedback

   Preachers can solicit written feedback targeted to specific areas on which they are working. One way of doing this is to craft a simple feedback form. Ushers can hand out a form and a pencil to five or six people at random as they come into Mass. These people return the form to the same usher as they leave. In this way, preachers do not know who is evaluating the homily and the parishioners can make comments anonymously. Preachers who do this at least once a liturgical season, or every few months, end up getting a clear picture from a cross-section of the community. The feedback form for this approach needs to be kept simple, but must capture what parishioners have heard, what resonates, what is effective and what needs work. Here are three examples.

Example 1

Thank you for giving feedback on the preaching at this Mass. Please fill out the form and return it to the usher as you leave.

1. What was the central message of the homily?

2. Where in the homily, if anywhere, did you hear the scriptures of this Mass applied to your life?

3. How could the preacher make the homily even better?

These three open-ended questions provide valuable information for preachers beyond a simple and ultimately unhelpful comment as to whether people liked the homily.

The first question asks them to put into words what they heard. It might surprise preachers to find out that what seemed crystal clear to them was not crystal clear to the listeners. It is a striking discovery to hear that several people each heard a different message. It may be, too, that the listeners do get a valuable message out of the homily; even if it was not the intended message, there has been some good done despite, not because of, the preacher. If the respondents use "and" several times in their answer to this first question, this might indicate that there is more than one message or pearl in the homily, as in "we are sent out after Mass to witness in our daily lives, and God calls us to repent and believe in the good news." A message calling the listeners to witness in their daily lives needs to be fleshed out, showing how to do that. A message calling listeners to repent and believe in the good news focuses on the interior spiritual life. Although certainly connected, each deserves its own homily. The assembly is not taking notes, and preachers cannot expect the listeners to work at holding together all the points of two messages.

The second question gets at a particular goal. It asks the listeners how well grounded in the scriptures they just heard they found this homily to be. In particular, it asks if the preacher clearly showed how these scriptures speak in the present tense, that is, relate to their lives. It is helpful when soliciting feedback on preaching outcomes like this one to get beyond a simple "yes" or "no" answer. Such answers do not tell the preachers very much. The open-ended structure of this question requires the listener to think of a primary example of where the preacher connected the proclaimed scriptures to contemporary experience. The kind of example chosen can inform the preacher of what makes his message more concrete.

The final question is also open-ended, giving the listener control of the form. The respondent now has the opportunity to raise an issue of importance to that person. The answers here are helpful because they can point out aspects of the preaching that the preacher might not have considered important or at issue. The respondent might note that slower or louder delivery is needed to make the homily clearer, whereas the preacher had no inkling this was a problem. It is from this question that the preacher can find out if there is something about his tone that puts the listener off. If one person makes such an observation, then the preacher knows that not everyone hears in the same way, and he can be more aware of how he preaches. If more than one person makes similar comments, the preacher has a target or goal for his preaching that he can incorporate into his next feedback form.

Example 2

I heard that the central message of this homily was:

_____

Was the homily firmly rooted in the scriptures of this liturgy?

☐ yes, firmly, because I heard _____

_____

_____

☐ some use of the readings, but not firmly rooted in them

☐ I did not hear much reference to the readings

Was this homily fully integrated with the liturgy?

☐ yes, because the preacher said _____

_____

☐ somewhat, but _____

☐ I did not hear a connection with the liturgy

Did this homily apply the scriptures to contemporary life?

☐ yes, when the preacher said _____

_____

☐ somewhat, but _____

☐ I did not hear a connection

Was this homily conversational?

☐ yes, because _____

_____

☐ somewhat, but _____

☐ I did not find it conversational

Was this homily centred on Christ?

☐ yes, because I heard _____

_____

☐ somewhat, but _____

☐ I did not hear Christ in this homily

Any additional comments

This form allows people to give feedback that is specifically linked to the marks of outstanding preaching highlighted in the Church documents reviewed in Part 1 of this book. It combines a check-off system with open-ended comments. It asks respondents who want to check "yes" indicating that the preacher has met the preaching competency to note briefly where and how that was done. That kind of feedback fleshes out the "yes" in a way that helps preachers determine exactly what worked in that homily. In this way, they know what connects and what to keep on doing.

Open-ended questions are most helpful for competencies around content. If preachers are particularly interested in feedback on delivery, a Likert scale will provide quick, measureable results.

Example 3

I found the audibility (volume) of the preaching

☐ Always audible

☐ Mostly audible

☐ Only sometimes audible

☐ I couldn't hear the preaching

I found the clarity (pronunciation and diction)

☐ Always clear

☐ Mostly clear

☐ Only sometimes clear

☐ I couldn't understand the preaching

I found the voice colour (change of pitch, inflection, emphasis) of the preaching

☐ Always engaging

☐ Mostly engaging

☐ Only sometimes engaging

☐ I wasn't engaged because there was little variety in the voice

---

I found the pace of the preaching

☐ Always well-paced

☐ Mostly well-paced

☐ Too fast

☐ Too slow

Any additional comments

Preachers can combine the various approaches described above or add other questions to craft a feedback form that focuses on their specific goals of improving preaching. They are no longer simply assessing themselves without the benefit of knowing how they are actually heard, and are saved from the well-meant but vague and ultimately unhelpful general comments at the church door after Mass.

4. Feedback Group

Oral feedback in a group setting can also give preachers useful input. These settings are more structured and less random than a feedback form handed out by ushers, filled out anonymously and then returned through the ushers to preachers. Here are two possibilities.

Feedback Group of Preachers

A small group of preachers committed to improving their preaching by inviting perspectives from each other can come together to discuss how they approached the same set of readings. The model of this approach is the Saginaw Program, put together by Bishop Ken Untener and described in detail in *Preaching Better* (2). As bishop of Saginaw, Michigan, he required his priests and deacons to discuss and give feedback on each other's homilies in a small group, of which he was a member. It worked like this.

1. Four priests, one deacon and the bishop formed a feedback group.

2. Each preacher, including the bishop, taped the upcoming homily and sent it to the bishop's assistant.

3. The bishop's secretary typed up transcripts, made copies of the recordings and sent a package to each person. Copies along with evaluation forms were also sent to six lay people not familiar with the preacher.

4. Each person listened to the tapes, read the transcripts and made notes.

5. All six group members and the director of communications came to a two-hour session in the bishop's office to give feedback to each preacher, beginning with the bishop.

This process was repeated three more times, at which time the bishop began a new group. If nothing else, such a commitment of time and energy demonstrates how seriously this bishop took preaching!

A group of preachers can form their own preaching feedback group, adapting the Saginaw Program to their own situation. Hearing how other experienced preachers handled the same readings and their perspectives on each other's homilies becomes a group-directed master class in preaching. Two hours a week in such a setting will produce the insights, help, support and thoughtful commentary to enrich each preacher's practice.

Feedback Group of Parishioners

Another possibility is a feedback group of parishioners. Like a feedback form, this method can be used once per liturgical season so that preachers hear how well they are connecting with their own communities. Preachers can select a number of people representing a cross-section of the parish.

The session can be structured in the following way.

1. Welcome and thanks. Restatement that the purpose of this group is to give feedback to the preacher on what was heard and how it was heard. The preacher needs to hear what is

already being done well and what can be done better in order to preach more effectively in the future.

2. Each person is asked to give a one-sentence reply: What was the message of this homily?

3. People are then invited to speak freely and in no particular order in response to this question: What did the preacher do well that he should keep on doing?

4. People are then invited to speak freely and in no particular order in response to this question: What could make this homily even better?

It is important for preachers not to get defensive. That is, they should resist the temptation to say, "Well, what I meant to say by that was…" or "I chose that story because…." This is not a place to justify what was done, but rather to find out how the homily was heard. The homilist's role in this group is not to tell the listeners how they should have heard it, but rather to evaluate how effectively the homily accomplished what was intended.

Preachers can favour one of these methods, use a combination of them, or devise a different one altogether until they find one that works well in their situation. The important thing is to find a way to listen to the listeners, to get concrete feedback on how the preaching was heard, to affirm preachers in what they are doing well, and to help them do better with the marks of outstanding preaching as their guide. In this way, in answer to Pope Benedict's observation, the quality of homilies will improve.

Part 3

Nuts and Bolts

Once preachers have a clearly developed theology of preaching framed with the expectations of the Church and a focused set of outcomes or competencies of outstanding Catholic preaching, the question remains: How do preachers do it all? It may seem overwhelming. So much is asked of them, all to be accomplished in 10 minutes. Although there is no single prescribed practice for attaining the marks of good preaching, there are good practices that preachers can consult. These good practices come from the experience of seasoned preachers and are implied by what the Church says it wants in the homily. None of the practices described in this part of the book are meant to be prescriptive, only helpful. In the end, they must build upon the qualities and style individual preachers bring to their calling.

The popes have consistently emphasized that preparation is not to be rushed and, moreover, that preachers have a method of preparation to which they devote significant time. By this the Church does not mean a great chunk of time carved out in one sitting, a day or two before preaching, but rather, as Pope Francis has called for, "a prolonged time of study, prayer, reflection and pastoral creativity" (*Homiletic Directory*, 26). Mary Margaret Pazdan, OP, in the Dominican tradition, breaks down the development of a homily into *contemplo*, *studeo* and *praedico*. Preachers using this practice put prayer first, consultation of resources second, and crafting the homily third.

Contemplo

The *Homiletic Directory* underscores the primacy of prayer in preparation, calling it "essential"; it continues, "the homily will be delivered in a context of prayer, and it should be composed in a context of prayer" (26). Bishop Fulton Sheen's practice of preparing his preaching in front of the Blessed Sacrament is an example of an important principle. Rather than making homily preparation another task added on to what preachers do, it can bear much fruit if it becomes part of daily spiritual practice. That is, preachers bring the texts of the liturgy to their daily prayer, adoration and meditations. They make their prayer time connected to their preaching. Both Pope Francis and Pope Benedict XVI have advised preachers to ask what the readings speak to them personally and then what they speak to the particular community to whom they preach. It is in the context of daily spiritual practice that these questions can be asked.

One method commonly recommended is *Lectio Divina*, a slow, prayerful reading of scripture. Pope Benedict describes the process as involving *lectio*, a slow reading to understand the content; *meditatio* to uncover what the scripture says to the preacher and his community; *oratio* to discover the words of response to the scripture; *contemplatio* to discern what conversion those scriptures are asking of us; and *actio* to determine what action the believer now needs to take. Such a process does not all happen in one sitting. If preachers begin preparing a week before, this first stage can take several days. It is valuable to make appointments with scripture to provide adequate time for this kind of *lectio*, but it will most certainly affect the rest of their time. Once questions have been raised, once preachers have opened themselves to the scriptures and prayed that the scriptures will be open to them, everything in their day becomes interpreted through them. Every event and conversation suddenly becomes an opportunity to understand what God is saying to them and to the community. What might have been passed over before in daily life becomes part of the school of homily preparation. Dedicated spiritual practice in assigned times of prayer on the scriptures seeps into everything and surfaces at unexpected moments, in the middle of the night, while engaged in one activity or another.

The US bishops, in the beautiful document *Fulfilled in Your Hearing*, call for an intriguing variation of *Lectio Divina*. They argue for a lectionary preparation group of parishioners engaging in a group *lectio* with the preacher. Although many contemplative methods are possible, this approach is so esteemed by the bishops that it is the only one described in detail. It is, in effect, a lectionary study that prepares both the listener and the preacher for the upcoming Sunday. The bishops outline the following process (*Fulfilled in Your Hearing*, 38):

Read the passages	15 minutes	One participant reads the passages out loud slowly.
Share the words	10 minutes	Each person shares the words or phrases that stood out without explanation.
Exegete the texts	10 minutes	One participant presents a short exegesis.
Share the good news	10 minutes	Participants share the good news from the readings.
Share the challenge	10 minutes	Participants discuss what the passages call us to and name the sins, pains and fractures which these readings touch.
Explore the consequences	15 minutes	Participants discuss the implications of applying the scriptures to their lives and the world.
Give thanks and praise	5 minutes	Concluding prayer of thanks for the Word.

This group *lectio* provides advantages to preachers who have already spent time praying their own *Lectio Divina*. This setting gives them an opportunity to hear which words or phrases from the scriptures of the upcoming Mass resonate with the listeners. They hear also what constitutes good news, what challenges and what may be problematic. Finally, they hear how the scriptures touch members of their community through example and story. Preachers can, on occasion, even ask permission from someone who has given a particularly powerful example if that story can be incorporated into the preaching. Preachers who use this method on a regular basis can ask anyone in the group who might be leaving to recruit a replacement, thus guaranteeing fresh perspectives.

Another method for *contemplo* is *scrutatio*, a method practised by the Neo-Catechumenate movement. As with the group *Lectio Divina* proposed by the US bishops, this method involves several people coming together to read through the scripture texts of the upcoming Sunday Mass. This prayerful reading is focused on tracing the threads of the text through all of scripture. For that, participants use the New Jerusalem Bible, which includes column references to ideas, words and themes found in other books of the Bible. Each participant prayerfully traces all the echoes throughout scripture by reading the other texts to which the references point. After meditating on what all of this as a totality says to the reader, anyone who wishes to do so stands to give a reflection on whatever insights have come to them. If practised on one's own, this method gives a richer sense of the context of scripture as a whole of Christ present in both testaments. If practised in a group, particularly with other preachers, it gives an opportunity to hear considered reflections and different perspectives on the Mass readings.

Studeo

An extended *contemplo* gives way to *studeo*, which is a consultation of what the tradition of the Church says about the readings. This critical stage needs to follow, rather than precede, *contemplo*. To look at resources before praying over the scripture makes other people's reflections prominent, which can filter out insights that can come from a dedicated listening to scripture. One temptation connected with putting *contemplo* first is to skip *studeo* altogether. That is, preachers listen to the scriptures in *contemplo* and then rush to get the fruits of that prayer down on paper. This can make the homily solely the fruit of a personal meditation. The assembly, however, deserves to hear preachers preaching in the name of the Church rather than in their own name. Consulting the whole tradition of the Church, ancient and modern writers, theologians and dogma ensures that the insights preachers pass on are consistent with Church teaching. *Studeo* can yield clarifications, explanations and examples, especially from the lives of the saints.

Each preacher will develop a list of personal favourite resources to turn to after *contemplo*. That list is most valuable when it takes into account both traditional and modern sources, so that preachers are informed by the continuing experience of the Church. Such a list could include

> ❯ a study Bible with extensive commentary notes
> ❯ a Catholic commentary series on scripture
> ❯ online sources that provide historical, patristic, modern and other interpretive perspectives on the readings for each Sunday
> ❯ resources like St. Thomas Aquinas' *Catena Aurea,* which provides commentary by the early Church Fathers on the gospels, verse by verse

In addition to consulting text sources like these, preachers will often find it valuable to look at paintings of particular events. Just as writers have contributed their insights in print, painters have contributed theirs by envisaging the event. The 15th-century painting of the Annunciation by Fra Angelico, for example, merges the expulsion of Adam and Eve from the garden with the Angel Gabriel's visit to Mary, as he brings the message that she will bear the Christ child. The painting shows that at the same moment that an angel drives humanity out, another angel comes with the news of reconciliation. The hand of God above the garden of Eden sends out the Holy Spirit in a ray of light that pierces time and enters Mary. This bringing together of Old Testament and New Testament in a single image is a powerful meditation for preachers.

Studeo can also involve gaining a better understanding of a contemporary event upon which scripture has something to say to us. After a *contemplo* on the tower of Siloam, for example, preachers might want to look into the details of modern disasters like the sinking of the *Titanic* or the attack on the World Trade Center on September 11, 2001.

Praedico

Having prayed with scripture and consulted resources, preachers then bring the threads they have into one place. The first thing that will help both preachers and listeners is to focus on what Bishop Untener called "the pearl" – a single idea for the homily. A homily that is too rich, with more than one main idea and several sub-points, loses its power to connect in a memorable way. The average listener is not taking notes. In fact, preachers should not expect their communities to work at listening to the homily. Some might, but it is not an expectation that preachers can reasonably hold for anyone. A single message powerfully driven home with a main image through concrete rather than abstract language makes a homily effective.

Thomas Long offers the preacher help by recommending a method that sets out what he calls "compass settings" for preaching. That method involves crafting two short statements: a focus statement and a function statement (Long, 86).

The focus statement

The focus statement provides the message of the homily. A word or two will not do because they will only announce a subject or a topic. A full sentence will provide the controlling idea, the main message that the preacher wants to convey. It is a valuable experience when collecting feedback, as described in Part 2 of this book, to see how closely the listeners' perceived focus statement matches the preacher's.

A useful device in constructing a focus statement is to avoid the word "and." Using "and" often signals that the preacher is bringing in a second idea. A response from a listener like "The preacher told us to never lose faith even in the midst of afflictions, and that our penances can bring us closer to Jesus who saves us, and that our mission is to carry out the Gospel in our words and our actions" is telling the preacher that several different things were heard. The points may or may not be related, but more than one message is competing for attention. Cardinal Newman insisted that preachers avoid piling on idea after idea – and in fact advocated for a single idea, or what he called "a bull's eye." "As a marksman aims at the target and its bull's-eye, and at nothing else, so the preacher must have a definite point before him, which he has to hit" (Newman, Lecture VI, part 2). Allowing in more than one idea not only weakens the effectiveness of the homily and strains the willingness of the assembly to work at listening but, Cardinal Newman maintains, also can ruin a homily.

> Nothing is so fatal to the effect of a sermon as the habit of preaching on three or four subjects at once. I acknowledge I am advancing a step beyond the practice of great Catholic preachers when I add that, even though we preach on only one

at a time, finishing and dismissing the first before we go to the second, and the second before we go to the third, still, after all, a practice like this, though not open to the inconvenience which the confusing of one subject with another involves, is in matter of fact nothing short of the delivery of three sermons in succession without break between them. (Lecture VI, part 2)

Sir Arthur Thomas Quiller-Couch, in his 1916 book *The Art of Writing*, advised writers to "murder their darlings." He calls for writers to strip out text that is not essential, that is ostentation, and that, in the end, satisfies the pride of the writer rather than the need for clarity. Guerric DeBona, OSB, applies this idea to homiletics. Preachers who have fully engaged in a *contemplo* and a *studeo* will often have mined many rich insights – but what has been gained over a week should not all be compressed into a 10-minute homily. One treasure at a time is enough. DeBona puts it this way:

Homilists may have lovely "children" that they have brought to light and want desperately to share with the congregation. Put these jewels away and hide them in a box on an index card for another homily. (80)

Preachers will find it useful to stand back from their preaching and question every idea, image or example. Is it there because it is dear to the preacher rather than necessary for the clarity of the pearl? If it is a tangent to that main message or a display of erudition, then it needs to come out.

The function statement

After preachers craft the focus statement, Thomas Long advocates for writing a function statement: putting into one sentence what the homily is meant to achieve, what effect it is meant to have. Homilies do not simply hold information; they make a claim on the listener. They intend to make a difference. The preacher might be out to move people to repentance, to reconciliation, to witness or to something else. The message of the homily is meant to cause a change. The Word of God is sent out and it is not supposed to return void. What, then, does the preacher intend to happen?

Putting focus and function statements side by side helps preachers know if they are on target. It will show them if they have a single pearl, which is a point worth making that has a clear aim at making a difference in the listener. Thomas Long raises three principles around these statements:

1. They should grow directly out of the exegesis of the biblical text.

2. They should be related to each other.

3. They should be clear, unified and relatively simple. (86–89)

Organizing the content

With a clear message and purpose in mind, preachers need a method to organize their homilies. Organization unifies a homily, making it stronger, clearer and memorable. The method can change from homily to homily, and from preaching situation to preaching situation. There is no single method for this – but it is important to have a method. St. Francis De Sales, in his book *On the Preacher and Preaching*, puts a high value on it: "We must adhere to method in all things; there is nothing that is more helpful to a preacher, makes his preaching more profitable, and so pleasing to his hearers" (53). He insists that the method should be "clear and evident." He then proceeds to suggests several different methods, all of which he uses, to organize the homily.

A helpful method has come into Catholic preaching from the New Homiletic movement that began in the 1970s in North America, principally from the work of Fred Craddock, Bandy Distinguished Professor of Preaching at Candler School of Theology at Emory University in Atlanta. A traditional model of preaching, normally named deductive preaching, presents the message, supporting points and a closing. It is sometimes described as three points and a poem. This structure is analogous to most academic writing, which presents a thesis, demonstrates it and then concludes. Craddock proposes a different model: an inverted model that distinguishes preaching from the academic approach. He proposes an inductive model. The preacher does not begin with the intended message, the thesis, but takes the listener step by step to the message that is uncovered or revealed at the end, the climax, of the preaching. In this way, the listener accompanies the preacher in search of meaning rather than having it laid out in front of him or her as a *fait accompli.*

Since then, several preachers have developed methods to frame an inductive homily. A particularly helpful one was developed by Dr. Eugene Lowry, a former professor of preaching at Saint Paul School of Theology in Kansas City. In *The Homiletical Plot*, Lowry outlines his method of organizing a homily along inductive lines (27–80).

Stage 1: Upsetting the Equilibrium

In this stage, preachers present a reason for listening by introducing an ambiguity, a problem or a question. One way to do this is to articulate the concerns, doubts and questions that the community has. It might be about the text itself (How could God actually ask a horror like Abraham killing his own son? What do you mean, "wives obey your husbands"? How far would I really get in the world if I always turned my cheek?). A good practice for preachers is that if they stumble over a text or find it perplexing or even unacceptable, then that is the place to start. If they run lectionary study groups as described above, they will hear questions and observations from the community that need to be taken seriously in the homily.

Stage 2: Analyzing the Discrepancy

This stage asks "why?" Preachers begin to look at the possibilities, including what comes from their experience or the experience of the listeners. Lowry advises preachers about this stage:

> Simply, it is to ask why and not be content with your answers. As you continue to reject each answer with another why, you will find increasing depth in your analysis, until you come across a reason underneath which you cannot go. (47)

The community finds itself accompanying preachers in this analysis because they hear their own concerns, their own thinking vocalized.

Stage 3: Disclosing the Clue to Resolution

Having looked at and explored the problem or ambiguity in a number of ways, preachers then find what Lowry likes to call the "aha!" moment. It is a key, perhaps a hint, a way of looking at the issue in a different way and from a fresh perspective that opens it up to make it more accessible. It comes as a discovery and a surprise. Lowry notes that it often functions as "a principle of reversal," turning the ambiguity or problem upside down in order to seek out some kind of resolution. That key can come from different places, but Catholic preachers can look to the whole body of readings and liturgical texts for the Mass. A line from the responsorial psalm, the collect or the preface to the Eucharistic prayer can be the glimmer that points preachers and their listeners to what the texts are all about.

Stage 4: Experiencing the Gospel

The first three stages take the listener through an articulation of the problem, wrestle with unsatisfying answers and glimpse a possibility. Having discovered the key to the upset at the beginning of the homily, preachers now expand on it, develop it and flesh it out as Good News. The whole problem now looks different. It can be understood in a way that was not possible before in the light of faith and the teachings of the Church – in other words, in Christ. Preachers uncover the light of the Gospel perspective in this part of the homily so that listeners have the experience of that light dawning upon them, helping them to make some sense of it all that they did not have before.

Stage 5: Anticipating the Consequences

The final stage of this homiletic method is to elaborate on the implications of the understanding that comes after discovering a key to the conundrum and experiencing the Gospel. What does it mean for the lives of the listeners in the modern world? Lowry puts it this way: "The last phase of the sermon articulates the possible consequences which now – thanks be to God – can be anticipated" (87). For Catholic preachers, this is the opportunity to take seriously the Church's call for prophetic preaching – preaching that holds up scripture as a lens to the world and in particular to the contemporary lives of the listener. It is here that preachers remember most particularly that they are preaching in the present tense.

The Lowry loop is only one of many possible methods. Preachers will find good models to use for method in many places and from many preachers. Paul Scott Wilson's four-page method in *The Four Pages of the Sermon* and Fr. Peter Cameron OP's eight-minute guideline in *Why Preach?* are only two examples. Preachers will also find their own methods or principles of organization that they will apply at different times to different homilies. Preachers should avoid using a single method slavishly, or else it becomes a repetitive formula and robs the preaching of its power by making it predictable. The idea in this part of *praedico* is simply to sit back, look at the content and be able to state a good reason why content material is where it is so that it serves the whole in an effective and memorable way.

Writing and delivering

Writing out the homily fully is a valuable step in *praedico*. It gives preachers the experience of finding the words, evaluating the organization and construction, and getting a good sense of their timing. Once they have done this, however, it is well worth trying to preach without the text. This is not to advocate memorization, which can render a homily stilted and mechanical by putting preachers on a train track; if they get derailed, it can be hard to get back on track. The idea is to aim for a delivery that is not concerned with being word perfect, but rather idea perfect.

Stepping into a pulpit for the first time with a thorough *contemplo* and *studeo* under one's belt, but without a text in hand that holds it all together, can be a daunting experience. In fact, it can be terrifying. Once they have tried it – or perhaps once they have gotten used to it, preachers will find that this approach gives them and their listeners wonderful benefits.

The first benefit is *focus*. Needing a manuscript at the ambo is often a sign that preachers have put too much content into their homilies. They are afraid of forgetting something, such as one of the sub-points or illustrations, and so they want the text in front of them. An oft-told story of a little old lady and Archbishop Fulton Sheen (there are so many stories about little old ladies and preachers) is that when seeing the famous preacher approach the pulpit with a stack of papers, she remarked, "Glory be to God! If he can't remember it, how does he expect us to?" This observation becomes good advice. By abandoning a manuscript, preachers preach on what is memorable for them, which in turn becomes memorable for the assembly. Preachers find that their homilies become more focused, more centred on the one pearl. They let go of the extraneous, the darlings, the sub-units, the ostentation and the complexities that might work in writing but do not suit an oral delivery.

The second benefit is brevity. The Church has promoted a short rather than a lengthy homily at Mass. When preachers have fully prepared, worked through the organization and possible wording of the homily, and then committed to giving it without the text, they often find that their focused homily is more brief because it is more pointed. Knowing that they will not use the text, they write a text that is leaner to begin with. It becomes a text that is easier to follow because it has jettisoned extra material, is more tightly wound and is easier to remember.

The third benefit is that it is more conversational. By distancing themselves from a text, preachers distance themselves from the habits of formal, academic language – especially if they have become accustomed to writing papers at a seminary. By no longer being concerned about having the exact choice phrases polished in the text, but rather aiming to be faithful to the flow of the homily, preachers are freed from trying to recreate the text or bring to memory perfect wording. They move from one part of the homily to the next, speaking directly to the assembly in familiar language, making eye contact and using more animated gestures. The issue is not to be concerned with this or that stumble in speech. Stumbles are, in fact, part of the regular cadence and tapestry of conversation. The issue is to keep a momentum animated by conviction and guided by the prayer and preparation that have gone into crafting a coherent message. Preachers who take the plunge to preach without notes often find that their homilies become more direct, even more intimate, because they are not tied to a text through which they mediate themselves to the listener.

A fourth benefit is a reliance on images and stories. Preaching without a text lends itself to the use of strong imagery and story. A strong image is easy for the preacher to remember and is memorable for the listener. A short narrative used as an example or illustration unfolds from itself. Not only does it serve to make abstract points concrete, it helps stitch the homily and preaching that appears effortless because it flows naturally. All of these qualities – concreteness, effortlessness and naturalness – enhance preaching and are fully consistent with what the Church asks of its preachers. Both image and story are natural fits for homilies that move away from several abstract ideas to single, more concrete ideas.

A method for preaching without notes

How, then, do preachers who have decided to preach without notes go about it – especially if the method is not to be memorization? One means of doing this is through the use of the Memory Palace.

The Memory Palace

The Memory Palace comes from classical Greek oratory. It is based on the idea that it is easier to remember places than random items or ideas. The Greek poet Simonides of Ceos was able to remember the details of where people had been after the collapse of a banquet hall. Sense of place is strong, particularly places with which we have solid connections, like our own homes. The Memory Palace technique is to link ideas or images in oratory sequentially to a place the speaker knows well. The Jesuit Matteo Ricci promoted this method in his missionary work in China, where scholars and students were eager to find effective ways to remember material for the examinations required for official posts.

After preachers finish writing their homily, they can reduce it to a series of moves, with each one connected to an image to create an internal storyboard. Each panel of that mental storyboard evokes an entire section of the homily. The key is to connect these images in a way that preserves the sequence and is memorable. Preachers can then use a familiar place, such as their own homes or the church building, on which to peg that sequence. Mentally walking through the place they have chosen, they put the images in various places as they go.

The following example shows how a homily can be broken into moves with assigned images, which are then attached to a familiar place, the preacher's home.

Moves from a Homily on the Holy Family	Image	Place (the preacher's home)
The first move or section of the homily has something to say about the Holy Family in Nazareth. The homily refers to the Collect. It describes the Holy Family, but then from the perspective of the listener challenges that scene as a model for us because it is so atypical. Mary is conceived without original sin, Jesus is God, and Joseph was a saint – and thus seemingly not like our family experience at all.	Christmas nativity scene	A nativity scene is outside the front door of the house.
The second move is a discussion of ideal family life – the kind of images we are given in the media, and the kind we imagine to be proposed by the Church for use. The model includes Mass attendance together, the family rosary and other devotions.	A Norman Rockwell painting of a family around the Thanksgiving table.	The door opens to reveal the painting hanging on the wall in the hallway.
The third move is a discussion of the realities that so many families face, including marriage break-up or children abandoning the faith, that cause great suffering to those in the family who are committed to the faith.	A newspaper with a headline or pie chart on the front page announcing the dissolution of the family.	The newspaper is lying below the painting on the hall table.
The fourth move brings the listener to the scriptures of the Mass, showing the grace of God at work in family life.	A bookstand with an open bible on it.	The bookstand is in front of the window of the main room.
The fifth move is the story of St. Monica and her faithful persistence in prayer for her husband, mother-in-law, and son, who became St. Augustine.	A statue of St. Monica	The statue is standing prominently in the middle of the floor of the first room of the house.

Moves from a Homily on the Holy Family (continued)	Image	Place (the preacher's home)
The sixth move offers some resolution. This move refers to the Prayer over the Offerings. The listener is not called to feel a sense of guilt or failure, but rather to trust, to be personally faithful, persistent with God and patient with family members on their own journeys.	An image of praying hands or of lighting a candle in prayer for others.	A lit devotional candle beside a small sculpture of the praying hands is on the mantelpiece beyond the statue.

All that is required after the preacher has fixed these images to particular places as in the chart above is to take a mental walk through the house during the preaching.

> The preacher comes up the veranda stairs and sees the nativity scene and says what scripture, *contemplo* and *studeo* have revealed for this preaching.

> After opening the door, the preacher sees the Rockwell painting and speaks of the various ideals that are presented to all of us.

> But then the mental eye of the preacher goes down to the table to read the newspaper headlines, bringing preacher and assembly face to face with the fact that things are far less than ideal – and that some people suffer for that, even feel guilt or failure at not being in an ideal family situation. It is a problem, and for many is a shared experience that needs some help.

> The preacher finds the open bible on the bookstand. Ribbons mark the readings of this Mass.

> The preacher sees this help walking into the living room and coming across the statue of St. Monica. Here is a story of a great saint and how she lived her faith in a family that was not ideal. The preacher is reminded of Monica's husband, her mother-in-law and her wayward son – and most of all is reminded of how St. Monica's

resolute faith, persistence and hope won the conversion of all of them in God's way and in God's good time.

- Finally, the preacher sees the lit candle and calls everyone to the same kind of generosity, love and patience for their family members. It is a faith and concern that never gives up – and that bears fruit in God's own kingdom.

An alternative to using place in this way for these images is to simply construct a mental art gallery and stroll by each painting or sculpture one by one. The advantage of the former method is that it firmly keeps sequence in place by connecting it to the familiar.

Starting and ending a homily

Starting the homily

Preachers sometimes ask for feedback on how effective their introductions and conclusions are. Thinking in those terms emphasizes an understanding of the homily as a separate piece. It can be helpful and liberating for preachers to realize that they do not have to think in that kind of framework. That is, they do not need to look for a device to grab attention, add exposition and make some kind of message or thesis statement, as in an essay or formal talk. Bishop Untener was blunt about this point:

> The first thing to say about beginnings is that homilies don't need one, that is, a specialized piece called a beginning. Some talks do, but homilies don't. Keep in mind that the liturgy already had a beginning (the gathering rite). (*Preaching Better*, 27)

He goes on to recommend that the preacher simply get right into it: "In a homily, the last thing we need is an attention getter" (22). The homily does not need an introduction, because it already flows out of everything that went before it. Discussing the relationship of the readings to the homily, the *Homiletic Directory* observes, "Both are proclamation, and this underscores once again how the homily is a liturgical act; indeed, it is a sort of extension of the proclamation of the readings themselves" (12). The Directory also discusses the importance of using the prayers of the Mass.

This point should not be overlooked, because the prayers provide a useful hermeneutic for the preachers' interpretation of the biblical texts. What distinguishes a homily from other forms of instruction is its liturgical content. (11)

Everything that preceded the homily, from the opening greeting to the last words of the Gospel, has established what an introduction would do in formal talk. They are, in fact, much more than an introduction, but rather moves in the liturgy of which the homily is one more.

That is why the homily does not need to open with a formal prayer or a sign of the cross. This has already happened; the homily is fully integrated with a movement that has already begun. Devices like jokes or stories that are meant solely for the purpose of warming up the audience waste the precious time of the homily and squander the energy that comes directly from the readings. That energy is also squandered if homily time is used retelling the events that were just proclaimed from scripture.

If preachers are using an inductive method, they can immediately address the problem – the upset on which the homily is focused. If preachers are using some other approach, they can get to the heart of the matter. That might be the pearl of the homily or the contemporary application in connection with or response to the biblical event.

Ending the homily

Just as the opening movements of the liturgy hand over to the movement of the homily, so the movement of the homily hands over to what follows in the liturgy. That is, it can be helpful for preachers to think in terms of handing over rather than concluding or ending. The homily does not end, but rather leads the listeners into the rest of the liturgy. At a baptism, the homily takes the people into the celebration of that rite. In the Mass, the homily takes the people into a deeper awareness of and attention to the Eucharist. Pope Benedict stressed that the homily was "to lead to an understanding of the mystery being celebrated" (*Verbum Domini*, 59). It does this first before it leads the listener to the *Ite Missa Est* – to living out the implications of the Gospel in their personal witness wherever they are outside of the Mass. Just as the homily does not need a formal sign of the cross to open it, neither does it need one to close it, because it does not close at all. Just as it flowed out of the early moves of the Mass, it flows into the later moves of the Mass, in which it is fully integrated.

Preachers can make references to the prayers or responses that will soon be said that bear upon the focus of the homily. They can look forward to the grace of the sacrament, the hymn that will be sung at the offertory or the prayer after Communion as some examples of propelling the listener forward into the rest of the liturgy. Recalling the prayers emphasized earlier in the homily can be a significant moment for the listeners, who may be in the habit of moving through these prayers automatically, without really attending to them. This kind of approach stitches together everything in the liturgy – one flowing into and out of the other. The *Homiletic Directory* says:

> When the homily is understood to be an organic part of the Mass, it becomes clear that the preacher is asked to see the constellation of the readings and prayers of the celebration as crucial to his interpretation of the Word of God. (16)

What's more, this integration with all the parts of the Mass gives the homily its proper focus of pointing to the sacrament.

Finding a concrete image

Although preachers might have a series of mental images to remember the image, it is helpful for the assembly to have one dominant image. When parishioners are asked later in the day, "So what was the homily about?" it can be difficult to recall abstract ideas completely or accurately. It is much easier to recall an image: "Oh, the homily was about the house that needed cleaning." If the homily has used more than one image, these images can compete for attention. When the images have a common connection, that is less of a problem. The house built on sand and the house built on rock are intimately related, for example. Opting for a single dominant image that is concretely described with sensory detail leaves a strong key that evokes the entire message of the homily. These images can come from the liturgy or the liturgical setting itself.

One of the most beautiful images of the entire liturgical year is the service of light at the Easter Vigil. The deacon enters with the Paschal candle. The altar servers light their tapers from this great candle and pass that light on to others, who in turn pass it to even more people. A lesson is learned in the doing. When we give the light away, we have no less than we started, and in fact we see an increase. Taper by taper, the darkness is pushed back. It is still there, but pushed back witness by witness – all of whom received their light from "the light of Christ." So much can be done with an image like this one. It might be used on a Sunday throughout the year when the focus, or pearl, of the homily is on witnessing empowered by the spirit, by grace, by the power of Christ. After the homily, when someone is asked what it was about, that person can recall the image of the Paschal candle being brought in and then bring to mind the details, which helps them unpack the whole homily.

The church itself offers many ideas, such as the crucifix over the altar, a stained-glass window, the nativity scene set up at the side of the church for the Christmas season, the Advent wreath – all opportunities to fix an image in the listeners' minds. Preachers can also find images from daily life that make the point succinctly. Certainly, this is what Jesus did in the parables when he spoke of seeds, fish, harvests and wedding banquets. Preachers look for an image that is a key to remembering and understanding. Just as scripture uses phrases such as "the kingdom of heaven is like…," so preachers can, in preparing the homily, complete the sentence "the point of this homily is like…." The image that completes the sentence can then become fixed in the minds of the listeners through specific detail – how it looks or sounds. In *Evangelii Gaudium*, Pope Francis emphasized the use of image over story. Story, too, can have great value, as in the extended stories of Jesus, such as the parable of the prodigal son. They gain their value, however, from a central, memorable image. The father welcoming his son with tears and slipping a ring on his finger stays in our memory. That image evokes the story, which in turn evokes the point of the preaching.

Knowing the community

The *Homiletic Directory* makes the important observation about a key aspect of the homily. It states: "the homily is a dimension of ministry that is especially variable, both because of the cultural differences from one congregation to another, and because of the gifts and limitations of the individual preacher" (3). It recognizes that what needs saying to one community is different from what needs saying to another. Pope Benedict, in *Verbum Domini*, emphasized that the preacher needs to seek what should be said to the particular community in front of him in light of the concrete situation they are in (59). The question is: How do preachers get to know their communities in this way? The Church has been clear that there is preaching advice available that is good for any community. As we see in the *Homiletic Directory*, the Church is advocating for certain principles when it comes to preaching in the modern world – or in the new evangelization, or in the 21st century – or however it is named. Those principles have to do with the way modern people listen and what concerns them. Certain things that were well and good in a different time will not necessarily work as well in our time. It is easier to reach people by the use of a single pearl, the inductive model, and the focus and the function methods. When a pastor speaks to his flock, he speaks to the assembly collected around him with their own particular needs and worldviews. But how does he know what those particular needs and worldviews are? The question is a good one.

It is not as difficult to assess these as it may sound – it really means just deciding to pay attention. What qualities of a parish are quickly apparent? One parish might be full of energy. People pack all the special events. A lot of money has come in to pay for upgraded facilities. Various appeal goals are set high because they are realistic. Another parish might be tired out, with only a handful of people attending special events. Appeal goals are set low. Much work needs to be done – but raising the money for it and getting volunteer commitment is problematic. What can be said for a parish can be said for specific Masses. It is clear to a preacher, for example, that one Mass has more families and children – and can even support a children's liturgy – while another Mass time has no children; those gathered are fewer and are generally older; and so on. Sometimes Masses are set up to have a certain character. For example, the type of music for the different Masses also indicates the kind of assembly that gathers.

In addition to all this, as a preacher settles into a parish, that preacher gets to know what is going on, what the people are concerned about, what conflicts might exist, the personalities of individuals and even groups. A preacher in a city that depends on manufacturing for jobs, which is always nervous about plant closures, will have different issues than a parish in farm country, which is different from a suburban parish of a big city where most people are professionals. They have different concerns, and although the message of the Gospel is the same, what they need to hear, how they hear and so on need attending to.

Other things can help a preacher as well. The lectionary study group, as proposed by the US bishops in *Fulfilled in Your Hearing* and described in Part 2 of this book, gives the preacher a keen sense of how people hear the Word – and what they find to be challenging (38). Another thing to keep in mind is that the preacher is not always speaking to the entire assembly as the primary listener – sometimes, one constituency is the primary listener and the rest of the assembly is the secondary listener. For example, in one homily, the preacher is primarily speaking to parishioners with young children; in another, to people who are in the midst of a trial; in another, to people who have the means to give and help others; and so on. In that case, knowing specific people in the assembly, which happens over time, allows the preacher to think in terms of how that person, as a member of the particular constituency focused on in the homily, would hear the homily – and what that person, as indicative of that group, might need in terms of language, imagery and so on for the message to get through.

Using media

St. Augustine, in *De Doctrina Christiana*, argued for using all the devices and tools of rhetoric in preaching. That is, what classical rhetoricians knew was effective for communication should be in the service of the Word in evangelization of the world. Similarly, in modern times, the Church, far from shunning new methods of communication, in particular the media, has encouraged the use of all the tools available for the new evangelization. Pope Benedict XVI coined a term to understand the context in which we now live: "the digital continent." In his 2009 message for the 43rd World Communications Day, he said,

> Just as, at that time, a fruitful evangelization required that careful attention be given to understanding the culture and customs of those pagan peoples so that the truth of the gospel would touch their hearts and minds, so also today, the proclamation

of Christ in the world of new technologies requires a profound knowledge of this world if the technologies are to serve our mission adequately. It falls, in particular, to young people, who have an almost spontaneous affinity for the new means of communication, to take on the responsibility for the evangelization of this "digital continent."

Preachers have used various visual and audio digital technologies since the invention of the radio. Fr. Leslie Rumble in Sydney, Australia, broadcast *Question Box*, and Fr. Charles Carty in St. Paul, Minnesota, broadcast *The Catholic Radio Hour* in the early 20th century. They, along with Archbishop Fulton Sheen, were at the forefront of using new media. In more recent times, Mother Angelica and Bishop Robert Barron have used a wide range of media for apologetics, preaching and evangelization.

Whereas the Church has actively promoted preaching in media, it has not, at least up to the time of this writing, pronounced on media in preaching – which is a very different thing. Preachers in other faith traditions have adopted screens, PowerPoint and video. Some, but few, Catholic preachers have followed suit. Many bishops have taken a wait-and-see attitude. Are the fruits good? Are they bad?

In the absence of clear direction on the desirability (or undesirability) of using media in preaching, preachers can determine for themselves the value of using it just as they would evaluate any other decision. That is, is it consistent with the vision of preaching to which the Church is calling them? Preachers can ask some pointed questions to assess how they are planning to use such technology.

1. How do the media affect the length of the homily?

   The Church has consistently called for the Sunday homily to be brief. It is meant to convey a memorable point that has an effect. It is not meant to be over-rich, the way a lecture might be, requiring the close attention of note taking. Neither is the homily meant to outbalance the Liturgy of the Eucharist. Preachers need to assess if the video clips they want to use stretch their homilies so that brevity is sacrificed and the Liturgy of the Eucharist is eclipsed.

2. How do the media affect the personal quality of the homily?

   The person of the preacher is meant to come through in a heart-to-heart preaching that conveys commitment, conviction and urgency regarding the importance of the Word. These personal qualities of the preacher are the central means to point to Christ. Preachers need to determine at what point media become too prominent and displace the personal quality of the homily.

3. How do the media affect what the homily does?

   The homily is meant to be Christocentric in that it proclaims Christ, facilitating an encounter with him and what he does. Some media, such as PowerPoint, can sometimes move the homily to a more instructional, lecture style. The homily is not meant to be a catechetical class in the Rite of Christian Initiation, or an exegetical lecture in a Bible study. Preachers need to assess if their use of media is helpful in fulfilling the Church's vision of the homily, or if it primarily facilitates the imparting of information.

4. How do the media affect what the homily is?

   Preachers who approach their vocation with a clearly articulated theology of preaching have in view a picture of what they are setting out to do when they step before the ambo. The Church has described the various facets of that vision, declaring that the homily is, as part of the liturgy, an act of praise. Preachers need to assess if the media they want to use further this vision or serve more as entertainment and distraction.

5. How do the media affect the integration of the homily with the rest of the liturgy?

   One of the most significant fruits of the homiletic renewal has been seeing the homily as integral to liturgy. This principle has profound implications for the homily's content, structure and delivery. Preachers who use media in their preaching need to ask themselves if the media helps the homily integrate well with the liturgy as a whole, or makes the homily stand out from the liturgy.

These questions do not include whether the assembly will like the use of media, but the liking is not the measure of whether it should be done. Preachers must take into account the needs of the community to do what is called for, not what is simply wanted. They also take into account what their calling to the primary apostolate may require. In that case, they are not simply doing what pleases them, either. The use of media, like any other decision as to what to include in a homily, requires careful thinking.

The preaching spot

Preachers have some thinking to do when deciding on the spot from which they will preach. The most recent *General Instruction of the Roman Missal* says:

> The priest, standing at the chair or at the ambo itself or, when appropriate, in another suitable place, gives the homily. (136)

This is significant change from the 1975 Missal, which states flatly:

> The homily is given at the chair or at the lectern. (97)

Traditionally, the bishop preaches from the chair, as from the seat of his authority. Other preachers would go to the ambo, technically a place, but now identified with the stand on which The Book of Gospels is placed for proclamation. The addition of the phrase "or, when appropriate, in another suitable place" validates some other practices that are now seen in Catholic churches, such as preaching in front of the altar or moving about the sanctuary. Preachers are given the latitude to choose from these, but need to work through why they are making that choice.

Preaching at the ambo

There are both theological and practical reasons for making this choice. Theologically speaking, preachers may want to stay anchored in the spot where the Word is proclaimed. They want to emphasize that their preaching is the extension of the proclamation from the Book. Practically speaking, they may wish to quote from one of the readings and so have the text in front of them, or may want to have a place to keep their notes to refer to them.

Preaching in front of the altar

Preaching in front of the altar emphasizes the unity between the Liturgy of the Word and the Liturgy of the Eucharist. This approach highlights that the sacrifice of the Mass, pointing to the death and resurrection of Jesus, is the interpretive key for scripture and for all our experience as a people of God. Preachers may also choose this place as a way of stepping out from behind a physical barrier and becoming more visible and, by implication, more present to the assembly.

Moving about in the sanctuary

Preachers can decide to move around, using the ambo as a sort of anchor. This movement allows them to add some animation to their delivery and to move closer to different sides of the assembly. They can make connections with the altar, the crucifix and the ambo, returning there when needed – such as when they read a quotation from the text.

What about preaching from the aisles?

Some preachers have adopted the practice of leaving the sanctuary altogether. The intention is to get among the people, to be with "the smell of the sheep," as Pope Francis has said. Such preachers will see this as a way of furthering the conversational qualities of the homily that the Church calls for. There are problems with this approach, however. The first problem is visibility. The preacher in the sanctuary is easier to see from all corners of the church. The preacher who leaves the sanctuary and comes down the aisle is at times obstructed from view by the heads of people – or from a position that now requires people to twist, lean over or struggle to see him. It is best for the preacher not to expect the assembly to work at listening or paying attention. Coming into the crowd might initially attract attention, but that novelty can quickly wear off.

Another issue is that although the new GIRM does add "or another suitable place", it is questionable whether being in the aisles is "suitable." Elsewhere, the GIRM states:

> The priest may give the sign of peace to the ministers but always remains within the sanctuary, so as not to disturb the celebration. (154)

This instruction for the sign of peace indicates a principle – that the celebration is disturbed when the priest leaves the sanctuary. It indicates that the priest is not to leave the sanctuary to be among the people, even when it might seem appropriate, such as at the sign of peace. If the presider should not leave the sanctuary for that case, it is hard to see that the GIRM is making provision for a preacher to leave the sanctuary.

Preaching the daily homily

Much, if not most, of the instruction and advice in the Vatican documents on homilies relates to the homily in the Sunday Eucharist, where a homily is obligatory. At the same time, preaching at daily Mass is desirable. Many preachers wonder how to prepare for daily preaching while they are engaged in the extended process of preparing their Sunday homily.

One way to approach the daily homily is to think of one extended daily homily that goes throughout the week, rather than six individual ones. The Introduction to the Lectionary provides a helpful insight:

> In using the Order of Readings for weekdays attention must be paid to whether one reading or another from the same biblical book will have to be omitted because of some celebration occurring during the week. With the arrangement of readings for the entire week in mind, the priest in that case arranges to omit the less significant passages or combines them in the most appropriate manner with other readings, if they contribute to an integral view of a particular theme. (82)

The principle that preachers can take away from this passage is that rather than looking at isolated texts, they can look at the readings throughout the week as one extended proclamation. Such an approach affects how the preacher prepares the homily, which unfolds throughout the week. It can refer to yesterday and look forward to tomorrow. It is not six different messages, but one message rooted in the readings heard that day placed in the context of what is heard over several days.

Bishop Untener adds an interesting perspective to the preaching of the weekday homily. Rather than see the daily homily as a shorter version of the Sunday homily, but essentially pegged to it, he suggests that we flip the paradigm around. He encourages preachers to make their Sunday homilies learn from the daily homily which, by its nature, contains so much of what the Church asks for in the Sunday homily: a tight focus, a strong scriptural basis, brevity, and a less self-conscious delivery, among others (103).

Preaching apart from the Sunday celebration and the daily Mass

Whether it is for a funeral, a wedding, a baptism or a Mass for another special occasion, the principles for good preaching at the Sunday liturgy apply. Preachers are still meant to find a memorable, worthwhile message that arises from the scriptures and the prayers of the liturgy. They are still meant to incorporate the homily fully, so that it flows into the next action of that liturgy and draws the listeners into a deeper appreciation and celebration of the sacrament. The homily brings the scriptures to bear on what is before the assembly – whether that is death, marriage or the new life of baptism. That the homily is meant to be Christocentric, focusing on what Christ accomplishes, is a helpful guide in all of these cases. It explains why the Church insists that the funeral homily is not to be a eulogy. Certainly, the deceased person is spoken of, yet the homily is not focused on the deceased, but on what Christ has made possible, both for the deceased and for all of us. Similarly, for a wedding, the homily naturally speaks of the couple, but it is not all about the couple. It is rather about Christ, and what Christ makes possible when he is brought into the marriage. Through baptism, children enter a life of grace made possible and empowered by Christ, who sets them on the journey of the spiritual life and is also the goal of that journey.

One thing that preachers can keep in mind is that these special events give them special opportunities. The assembly at a funeral Mass listens in a way that regular Sunday churchgoers may not. This is particularly true in the case of a tragic death of a young person, or after a long illness. The people gathered have questions; they are already asking "why?" and looking for answers. They are primed to hear out a preacher with more attention, and likely for longer, than the preacher could normally expect on a Sunday morning. Marriages and baptisms typically bring the churched and the unchurched together, which creates a particular moment to plant the seeds of the Good News of Jesus Christ.

Afterword

Preaching as the primary apostolate requires grace. That is God's work. It also requires dedication, preparation and commitment. That is the preacher's work. At the same time, preachers do not do that work on their own, nor should they. They do it with the guidance of the Church, which sets out the parameters of Catholic preaching. Those parameters create the boundaries and the goals. They are clear and hold out the ideal.

Preachers work within those boundaries, reaching for those goals and ideals in their own individual ways, using the talents and personalities God has given them. To say that the Church has an articulated theology of preaching is not to say that all preachers must be alike or that all homilies should be the same. That would be disrespectful of both the preacher and the assembly. Rather, the unique qualities a preacher brings to preaching for a particular assembly are guided by what the Church wants for its people – anything less would be disrespectful of the Church.

Preachers who give their preaching pride of place in their ministry by preparing their homilies, bringing the scriptures to prayer, responding to the needs of the assembly, consulting the tradition of the Church, and attending to their delivery are a gift to all of us.

This book began with the promise and challenge of St. Paul that speaks to every preacher. It ends with that same promise and challenge, giving St. Paul the last word calling for grace-filled preaching of the Good News in the name of the Church for the salvation of the world:

For, "Everyone who calls on the name of the Lord shall be saved."
But how are they to call on one in whom they have not believed?
And how are they to believe in one of whom they have never
heard? And how are they to hear without someone to proclaim
him? And how are they to proclaim him unless they are sent?
As it is written, "How beautiful are the feet of those who bring
good news!" (Rom 10:13-15)

References

Augustine. *De Doctrina Christiana.*

Baldwin of Canterbury, Bishop. Office of Readings. Friday, Thirtieth Week in Ordinary Time.

Bellinger, Karla. *Connecting Pulpit and Pew: Breaking open the Conversation about Catholic Preaching.* Collegeville, MN: The Liturgical Press, 2014.

Benedict XVI. *Sacramentum Caritas* (On the Eucharist as the Source and Summit of the Church's Life and Mission), 2007.

Benedict XVI. *Verbum Domini* (On the Word of God in the Life and Mission of the Church), 2010.

Canadian Conference of Catholic Bishops. *Program for Priestly Formation*, 2002. https://secure.cccb.ca/pubs/pdf/184-093%20Priestly%20Formation.pdf

Carrell, Lori. *The Great American Sermon Survey.* Wheaton, IL: Mainstay Church Resources, 2000.

Catholic Association of Teachers of Homiletics. *The State of Homiletics in the Seminaries and Graduate Schools of Theology in the United States,* 2002.

CNN Belief Blog March 30, 2012. "7 Reasons Catholics leave church (in Trenton, #1 is sex abuse crisis)." http://religion.blogs.cnn.com/2012/03/30/7-reasons-catholics-leave-church-in-trenton-1-is-sex-abuse-crisis

Coleridge, H.E. Most Rev. Mark Benedict Archbishop of Canberra-Goulburn, Australia. Intervention at the Third General Congregation at the Synod of The Word of God in the Life and Mission of the Church (7 October 2008).

Congregation for Divine Worship and the Discipline of the Sacraments. *The Homiletic Directory*, 2015.

Debona, Guerric. *Preaching Effectively, Revitalizing Your Church: The Seven-step Ladder toward Successful Homilies.* New York: Paulist Press, 2009.

DeLeers, Stephen Vincent. *Written Text Becomes Living Word: The Vision and Practice of Sunday Preaching.* Collegeville, MN: Liturgical Press, 2004.

Dziwisz, H. Em. Card. Stanislaw Archbishop of Krakow. Intervention at the Sixth General Congregation at the Synod of The Word of God in the Life and Mission of the Church (9 October 2008).

Francis. *Evangelii Gaudium* (On the Proclamation of the Gospel in Today's World), 2013.

General Introduction to the Lectionary, 1981.

General Introduction to the Roman Missal (English Translation), 2010.

Greeley, Andrew. "For Priests, Celibacy Is Not the Problem," *The New York Times* (Opinion), March 3, 2004. http://www.nytimes.com/2004/03/03/opinion/for-priests-celibacy-is-not-the-problem.html

Harrahan, D.V. "Must We Have Sermons?" *Homiletics and Pastoral Review* 47 (1947) 333.

Instrumentum Laboris, Synod of The Word of God in the Life and Mission of the Church (2008), n. 27.

John Paul II. *Apostolorum Successores* (Directory for the Pastoral Ministry of Bishops), 2004.

John Paul II. *Catechesi Tradendae* (On Catechesis in Our Time), 1979.

John Paul II. *Redemptoris Missio* (On the Permanent Validity of the Church's Missionary Mandate), 1990.

Kicanas, H.E. Most Rev. Gerald Frederick Bishop of Tucson, Intervention at the Third General Congregation at the Synod of The Word of God in the Life and Mission of the Church (7 October 2008).

Long, Thomas. *The Witness of Preaching*. Louisville, KY: Westminster John Knox Press, 1989.

Lowry, Eugene. *The Homiletical Plot: The Sermon as Narrative Art Form*. Louisville, KY: Westminster John Knox Press, 2001.

Monshau, Michael. *Preaching at the Double Feast*. Collegeville, MN: Liturgical Press, 2006.

Newman, John Henry. *The Idea of a University*. London: Basil Montagu Pickering, 1873.

Ouellet, H. Em. Card. Marc Archbishop of Quebec. *Report Before the Discussion of the General Reporter*, Synod of The Word of God in the Life and Mission of the Church (October 2008). 2.A.b.

Paul VI. *Ecclesiam Suam* (On the Church), 1964.

Paul VI. *Evangelii Nuntiandi* (Evangelization in the Modern World), 1975.

Paul VI. *Mysterium Fidei* (The Mystery of Faith), 1965.

Paul VI. *Presbyterorum Ordinis* (Decree on the Ministry and Life of Priests), 1965.

PewResearch Religion & Public Life Project "Religious Landscape Survey" (March 18, 2015). http://religions.pewforum.org/reports

Ratzinger, Joseph (Benedict XVI). "Christocentrim in Preaching?" (Christozentrik in der Verkundigung?), in Michael Miller, ed., *Dogma and Preaching.* San Francisco: Ignatius Press, 2011.

Ratzinger, Joseph (Benedict XVI). "Contemporary Man Facing the Question of God" (Der Heutige Mensch vor der Gottesfrage), in Michael Miller, ed., *Dogma and Preaching.* San Francisco: Ignatius Press, 2011.

Rwoma, H.E. Most Rev. Desiderius Bishop of Tanzania. Intervention at the Fourth General Congregation, Synod of The Word of God in the Life and Mission of the Church (7 October 2008).

Sacred Congregation for the Sacraments and Divine Worship. *Inaestimabile Donum* (Instruction Concerning Worship of the Eucharistic Mystery), 1980.

Sacred Congregation for the Sacraments and Divine Worship. *Notitiae,* v. 9 (1978), 178, DOL-1432; note R8.

Sacrosanctum Concilium (The Constitution on the Sacred Liturgy), 1963.

Spadaro, Antonio. "A Big Heart open to God," in *America,* September 30, 2013.

United States Conference of Catholic Bishops. *Fulfilled in Your Hearing: The Homily in the Sunday Assembly.* Washington, D.C., 1982.

United States Conference of Catholic Bishops. *Preaching the Mystery of Faith: The Sunday Homily.* Washington, D.C., 2013.

United States Conference of Catholic Bishops. Program of Priestly Formation. Washington, D.C., 2006.

Untener, Ken. *Preaching Better: Practical Suggestions for Homilists.* New York: Paulist Press, 2002.

Waznak, Robert. *An Introduction to the Homily.* Collegeville, MN: The Liturgical Press, 1998.